W9-CZY-609

Jennifer Evans 2002

Jennifer Evans 2002

中国西安

陕西历史博物馆

王建时赠

二〇〇三年七月二十日

大唐壁畫

Magnificent Frescos from the Great Tang Dynasty

李國珍 編撰
Compiled by Li Guozhen

李國珍

2002.7.11

中國·陝西旅游出版社
Shaanxi Tourism Publishing House China

目次

CONTENTS

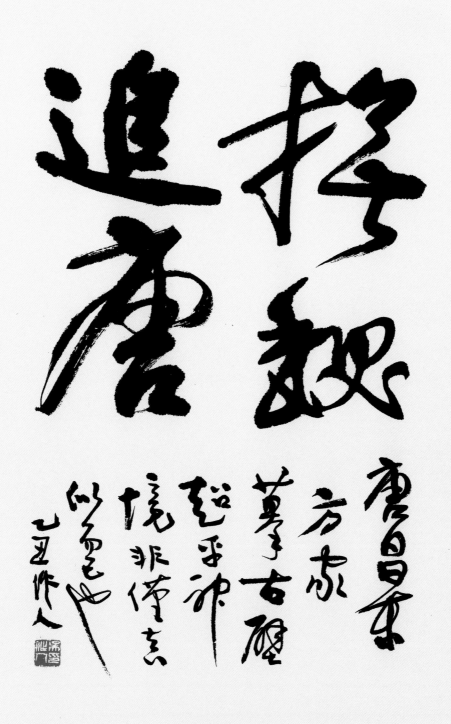

撫魏追唐　唐昌東方家摹古壁超乎神境　非僅真似而已也　乙丑作人（中國美術家協會主席、中央美術學院教授吳作人先生，1985 年題詞。）

In reflecting on the Wei in light of the Tang, it can be seen that the ancient frescoes copied by expert Mr. Tang Changdong and imitation are not the very images of the original paintings but are miraculously created, Zuoren 1985 (the chairman of the Chinese Artists Association, Professor of the Central Institute of Fine Art).

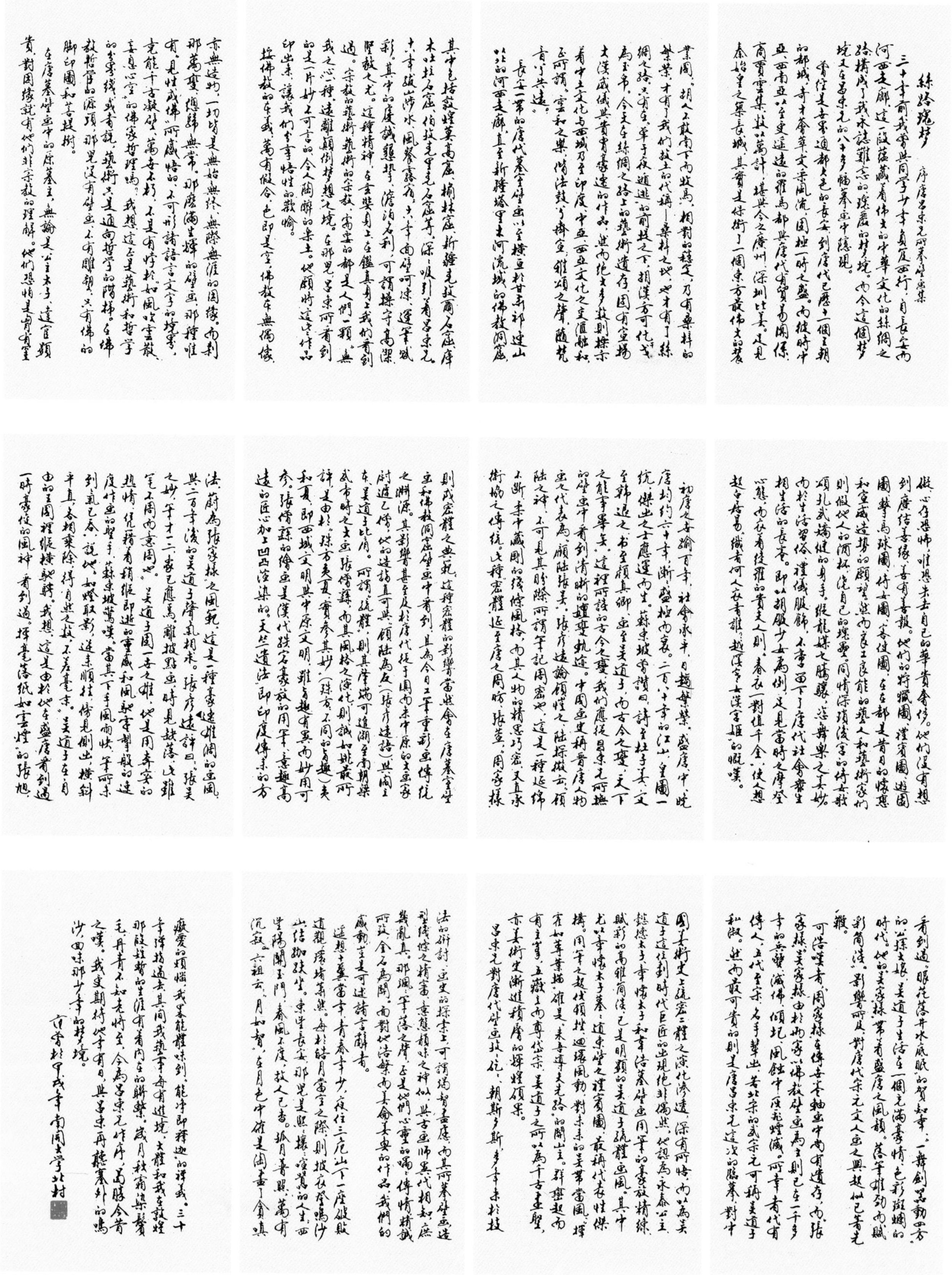

絲路瓊夢

序唐昌東先生所摹壁畫集

三十年前我曾與同學廿人負笈西行，自長安而河西走廊，這一段蘊藏着偉大的中華文化的絲綢之路構成了我永誌難忘的、瑰麗的夢境。而今這個夢境又在昌東兄的八十多幅摹畫中隱現。

曾經是古昔通都大邑的長安，到唐代已歷十一個王朝的都城，奇才薈萃，文采風流，固極一時之盛。而彼時中亞、西南亞以至更遙遠的羅馬都與唐代有貿易關係，商賈雲集，數以萬計，堪與今之廣州、深圳比美。足見秦始皇之築長城，其實是保衛了一個東方最偉大的農業國，胡人不敢南下而牧馬，相對的穩定，乃有桑梓的繁榮，才有了我們故土的代稱——桑梓之地，也才有了絲綢之路。只有在"單于夜遁逃"的前提之下，胡漢方可化干戈為玉帛。今天在絲綢之路上的藝術遺存，固有宣揚大漢威儀與貴胄豪邁的作品，然而絕大多數則標示着中土文化與西域乃至印度、中亞、西亞文化之交匯融和，正所謂"雲和之樂，偕法鼓於禪室；雅頌之聲，隨梵音以共遠"。

長安一帶的唐代墓室壁畫以至橫亘於甘肅祁連山以北的河西走廊，直至新疆塔里木河流域的佛教洞窟，其中包括敦煌莫高窟、榆林窟、新疆克孜爾石窟、庫木吐拉石窟、伯孜克里克石窟等，深深吸引着昌東兄。十六年跋山涉水、風餐露宿，六年面壁呵凍、運筆賦彩。其中的虔誠懇摯、澹泊名利，可謂操守高潔、堅毅之尤。這種精神，在玄奘身上，在鑒真身上我們看到過。宗教的藝術，藝術的宗教，寄寓的都是人們一顆"無我之心"，一種"遠離顛倒夢想"之境。在那兒，昌東所看到的是一片妙不可言的、令人陶醉的樂土。他願將這些作品印出來，讓我們去享悟性的歡愉。

按佛教的本義，萬有假合，色即是空，佛教本無偶像，亦無造物，一切皆是無始無終、無際無涯的因緣。而剎那萬變，總歸無常。那麼滿生輝的壁畫，那種唯有"見性成佛"所感悟的，不可形諸語言文字的境界，竟能千古凝碧，萬世不朽，不是有悖於"如風吹雲散、妄息心空"的佛家哲理嗎？我想這正是藝術和哲學的分野線，或者說，藝術只是通向哲學的階梯。在佛教哲學的源頭，那兒沒有壁畫，不有雕塑，只有佛的腳印圖和菩提樹。

在唐墓壁畫中的原墓主，無論是公主太子、達官顯貴，對因緣就有他們非宗教的理解。他們恐怕是有宣假，心存恐怖，唯恐失去自己的華貴奢侈。他們沒有想到廣結善緣，善有善報。他們的狩獵圖、禮賓圖、遊園圖、擊馬球圖、侍女圖、客使圖，在在都是昔日的懷戀和豪盛造勢的願望。然而宮工良能的藝人和藝術家們則假他人的酒杯，澆自己的塊壘。同情深埋後宮的侍女，歌頌孔武矯健的身手，縱龍媒之騰驤，盛舞樂之美妙，而於生活習俗、禮儀服飾，不啻留下了唐代社會衆生相生活的長卷。即以胡服少女為例，足見當時之摩登心態，而衣着綾羅的貴夫人則"春衣一對值千金"，使人想起白居易"織者何人衣者誰，越溪寒女漢宮姬"的慨嘆。

初唐之安逾百年，社會承平，日趨繁榮，盛唐、中、晚唐均約六十年，漸漸盛極而衰。二百八十年的江山，皇圖一統，傑出之士應運而生。蘇東坡曾讚曰：詩至杜子美，文至韓退之，書至顏真卿，畫至吳道子，而古今之變，天下之能事畢矣。這裡所談的古今之變，我們應從昌東兄所撫的壁畫中看到清晰的嬗變軌迹。中國畫史稱晉唐人物畫之代表為顧陸張吳。張彥遠論顧愷之、陸探微云"顧陸之神，不可見其盼際，所謂筆迹周密也"。這是一種延綿不斷、柔中藏剛的綫條風格，而其人物的精思巧密，又直承衛協之傳統。此種密體延至唐之周昉、張萱，"周家樣"則成密體之典範。這種密體的影響當然會在唐墓室壁畫和佛教洞窟壁畫中看到，且為今日工筆重彩畫傳統之淵源。其影響甚至及於唐代從于闐而來中原的大畫家尉遲乙僧，他的造詣直可與"顧陸為友"（張彥遠語），與閻立本、吳道子比肩。所謂"疏體"，則其濫觴可追溯至南朝梁武帝時之大畫家張僧繇，而其風格之演化，則誠如姚最所評，是由於"殊方夷夏，實參其妙"（殊方，不同的旨趣）。夷和夏，即西域文明與中原文明，雖旨趣有異而妙用可參。張僧繇的繪畫是漢代雄宕豪放的用筆、意趣高遠的匠心加上凹凸渲染的"天竺遺法"，即印度傳來的方法，蔚為"張家樣"之風範，這是一種豪邁雄闊的畫風。與二百年後的吳道子聲氣相求。張彥遠評曰"張吳之妙，筆才一二，象已應焉。離披點畫，時見缺落，此雖筆不周而意周也"。吳道子固一世之雄，他是用奔突的熱情，凭着稍縱即逝的靈感和風馳電掣般的速度作畫的聖手。蘇東坡驚嘆"當其下手風雨快，筆所未到氣已吞"。說他"如燈取影，逆來順往，傍見側出，橫斜平直，各相乘除，得自然之數，不差毫末"。吳道子在自由的王國裡縱橫馳騁。我想，這是由於他在盛唐看到過一時豪俊的風神，看到過"揮毫落紙如雲煙"的張旭，看到過"眼花落井水底眠"的賀知章，"一舞劍器動四方"的公孫大娘，吳道子生活在一個充滿豪情、色彩斑斕的時代。他的"吳家樣"帶着盛唐之風韻，落筆雄勁而賦彩簡淡。影響所及，對唐代宋元文人畫之興起似已著先鞭。

可浩嘆者，"周家樣"在傳世卷軸畫中尚有遺存，而"張家樣"、"吳家樣"由於兩家以佛教壁畫為主，則已在一千多年的兵燹、滅佛、傾圮、風蝕中灰飛煙滅。所幸者代有傳人，五代至宋，名手輩出，若北宋的武宗元可稱吳道子私淑。然而最可貴的則是唐昌東兄這次的臨摹，對中國美術史上疏密二體之演化滲透，深有所悟，而以為吳道子這位劃時代巨匠的出現絕非偶然。他認為永泰公主、懿德太子、章懷太子和韋浩墓壁畫用筆的豪放精練、賦彩的高雅簡淡，已是明顯的吳道子疏體畫風。其中尤以章懷太子墓墓道東壁之禮賓圖，最稱代表性傑構。用筆之起伏頓挫，迴環風動，對未來的"吳帶當風"，揮霍如蓴葉描，確是"來吾導夫先路"的開山之。群巒起而有主峯，五嶽立而尊岱宗，吳道子之所以為千古畫聖，亦美術史漸進積層的輝煌碩果。

昌東兄對唐代壁畫孜孜矻矻，朝斯夕斯，多年來於技法的研討、畫史的探索上，可謂竭智盡慮，而其所摹壁畫，造型綫條之精審，意態韻味之神似，與古畫師異代相知，庶幾亂真。那颯颯筆落之聲，正是他們心靈的喁喁傳情，精誠所致，金石為開。面對他浩繁而美侖美奐的作品，我們的感動豈是可述諸言辭者。

遙想當年青春年少，夜住三危山下一座破敗道觀，環堵蕭然。每於皓月當空之際，則披衣登鳴沙山結跏趺坐。東望長安，那兒是熙熙攘攘喧囂的人生；西望陽關玉門，春風不度，故人已杳。孤月普照，萬有沉寂。六祖云"月如智"，在月色中確是消盡了貪嗔癡愛的煩惱，我嘗能體味到"能淨即釋迦"的禪義。三十年彈指過去，其間我藝事每有進境，大體和我在敦煌那段短暫的生涯有着內在的聯繫。歲月秋霜染鬢毛，丹青不知老將至，今為昌東兄作序，益勝今昔之嘆。我更期待他年有日，與昌東再聽塞外的鳴沙，回味那少年的夢境。

范曾於甲戌年南開大學北村

范曾手稿 The manuscript of Fan Zeng

絲路瑰夢
序唐昌東兄所摹壁畫集

范 曾

　　三十年前我曾與同學少年負笈西行，自長安而河西走廊，這一段蘊藏着偉大的中華文化的絲綢之路，構成了我永誌難忘的瑰麗的夢境。而今，這個夢境又在昌東兄的一百二十多幅摹畫中隱現。

　　曾經是世界通都大邑的長安，到唐代已歷十一個王朝的都城，奇才薈萃，文彩風流，固極一時之盛。而彼時中亞、西南亞以至更遙遠的羅馬都與唐代有貿易關係，商賈雲集，數以萬計，堪與今之廣州、深圳比美。足見秦始皇之築長城，其實是保衛了一個東方最偉大的農業國，"胡人不敢南下而牧馬"，相對的穩定，乃有桑梓的繁榮，才有了我們故土的代稱——桑梓之地，也才有了絲綢之路。只有在"單于夜遁逃"的前提之下，胡漢方可化干戈爲玉帛。今天在絲綢之路上的藝術遺存，固有宣揚大漢威儀與貴胄豪逸的作品，然而絕大多數則標示着中土文化與西域乃至印度、中亞、西亞文化之交匯融和，正所謂"雲和之樂，偕法鼓兮齊宣，雅頌之聲，隨梵音兮共遠"。

　　長安一帶和唐代墓室壁畫，以至橫亘於甘肅祁連山以北的河西走廊，直至新疆塔里木河流域的佛教洞窟，其中包括敦煌莫高窟、榆林窟、新疆克孜爾石窟、庫木吐拉石窟、伯孜克里克石窟等，深深吸引着昌東兄。十八年跋山涉水、風餐露宿；十八年面壁呵凍、運筆賦彩。其中的虔誠懇摯、澹泊名利，可謂操守高潔、堅毅之尤。這種精神，在玄奘身上、在鑒真身上我們看到過。宗教的藝術，藝術的宗教，需要的都是人們一顆"無我之心"，一種"遠離顛倒夢想"之境。在那兒，昌東所看到的是一片妙不可言的、令人陶醉的樂土。他願將這些作品印出來，讓我們分享悟性的歡愉。

　　按佛教的本義，萬有假合，色即是空，佛教本無偶像，亦無造物，一切皆是無始無終，無際無涯的因緣。而刹那萬變，總歸無常。那麼滿壁生輝的壁畫，那種唯有"見性成佛"所感悟的、不可形諸語言文字的境界，竟能千古凝壁、萬世不朽，不是有悖於"如風吹雲散，妄息心空"的佛家哲理嗎？我想，這正是藝術和哲學的分界綫，或者說，藝術只是通向哲學的階梯。在佛教哲學的源頭，那兒沒有壁畫、不有雕塑，只有佛的腳印圖和菩提樹。

　　在唐墓壁畫中的原墓主，無論是公主太子、達官顯貴，對因緣就有他們非宗教的理解。他們恐怕是胸有窒礙，心存恐怖，唯恐失去自己的華貴奢侈。他們沒有想到廣結善緣、善有善報。他們的狩獵圖、禮賓圖、游園圖、擊馬球圖、侍女圖、客使圖，在在都是昔日的懷戀和宣威造勢的願望。然而良工良能的藝人和藝術家們則假他人的酒杯，澆自己的塊壘。同情深鎖後宮的侍女，歌頌孔武矯健的身手。縱龍媒之騰驤，恣舞樂之美妙。而於生活習俗、禮儀服飾，不啻留下了唐代社會衆生相生活的長卷。即以胡服少女爲例，足見當時之摩登心態，而衣着綾羅的貴夫人則"春衣一對值千金"，使人想起白居易"織者何人衣者誰？越溪寒女漢宮姬"的慨嘆。

　　初唐之世踰百年，社會承平，日趨繁榮。盛唐、中、晚唐均約六十年，漸漸盛極而衰。二百八十年的江山，皇圖一統，傑出之士應運而生。蘇東坡曾讚曰："詩至杜子美，文至韓退之，書至顏真卿，畫至吳道子，而古今之變，天下之能事畢矣"。這里所談的古今之變，我們應從昌東兄所撫的壁畫中看到清晰的嬗變軌跡。中國畫史稱晉唐人物畫之代表爲"顧、陸、張、吳"。張彥遠論顧愷之、陸探微云："顧、陸之神，不可見其盼際，所謂筆記周密也"，這是一種延綿不斷、柔中藏剛的綫條風格，而其人物的精思巧密，又直承衛協之傳統。此種"密體"延至唐之周昉、張萱,"周家樣"則成密體之典範。這種密體的影響當然會在唐墓室壁畫和佛教洞窟壁畫中看到,且爲今日工筆重彩畫傳統之淵源。其影響甚至及於唐代從于闐而來中原的大畫家尉遲乙僧,他的造詣真可與"顧陸爲友"(張彥遠語),與閻立本、吳道子比肩。所謂"疏體",則其肇端可追溯至南朝梁武帝時之大畫家張僧繇,而其風格之演化,則誠如姚最所評,是由於"殊方夷夏,實參其妙"(殊方:不同的旨趣),夷和夏,即西域文明與中原文明,雖旨趣有異而妙用可參。張僧繇的繪畫是漢代跌宕豪放的用筆,意趣高遠的匠心加上凹凸渲染的"天竺遺法"即印度傳來的方法,蔚爲"張家樣"之風範,這是一種豪逸雄闊的畫風,與二百年後的吳道子聲氣相求。張彥遠評曰:"張、吳之妙,筆才一二,象已應焉。離披點畫,時見缺落,此雖筆不周而意周也"。吳道子固一世之雄,他是用奔突的熱情,憑籍着稍縱即逝的靈感和風馳電掣般的速度作畫的聖手,蘇東坡驚嘆:"當其下手風雨快,筆所未到氣已吞",説他"如燈取影,逆來順往,傍見側出,橫斜平直,各相乘除,得自然之數,不差毫末"。吳道子在自由的王國裡縱橫馳騁。我想,這是由於他在盛唐看到過一時豪俊的風神,看到過"揮毫落紙如雲煙"的張旭,看到過"眼花落井水底眠"的賀知章、"一舞劍器動四方"的公孫大娘,吳道子生活在一個充滿豪情、色彩斑爛的時代。他的"吳家樣"帶着盛唐之風韻"落筆雄勁而賦彩簡淡"。影響所及,對唐代宋元文人畫之興起似已著先鞭。

可浩嘆者"周家樣"在傳世卷軸畫中尚有遺存,而"張家樣"、"吳家樣"由於兩家以佛教壁畫爲主則已在一千多年的兵燹、滅佛、傾圮、風蝕中灰飛煙滅。所幸代有傳人,五代至宋,名手輩出,若北宋的武宗元可稱吳道子私淑。然而最可貴的則是唐昌東兄這次的臨摹,對中國美術史上疏密二體之演化滲透,深有所悟,而以爲吳道子這位劃時代巨匠的出現絕非偶然,他認爲永泰公主、懿德太子、章懷太子和韋浩墓壁畫用筆的豪放精練,賦彩的高雅簡淡,已是明顯的吳道子疏體畫風。其中尤以章懷太子墓墓道東壁之禮賓圖,最稱代表性傑構。用筆之起伏頓挫、迴環風動,對未來的吳帶當風,"揮霍如蓴葉描"確是"來吾導夫先路"的開山主。群巒起而有主峰,五嶽立而尊岱宗,吳道子之所以爲千古畫聖,亦美術史漸進積層的輝煌碩果。

昌東兄對唐代壁畫孜孜矻矻、朝斯夕斯,多年來於技法的研討,畫史的探索上,可謂竭智盡慮,而其所摹壁畫,造型綫條之精審、意態韻味之神似,與古畫師異代相知,庶幾亂真。那颯颯筆落之聲,正是他們心靈的喁喁傳情。精誠所致、金石爲開。面對他浩繁而美侖美奐的作品,我們的感動,豈是可述諸言辭者。

遙想十翼當年,青春年少,夜住三危山下一座破敗道觀,環堵蕭然。每於皓月當空之際,則披衣登鳴沙山,結跏趺坐。東望長安,那兒是熙熙攘攘喧囂的人生;西望陽關玉門,春風不度,故人已杳。孤月普照,萬有沉寂。六祖云:"月如智",在月色中確是淘盡了貪嗔癡愛的煩惱,我略能體味到"能淨即釋迦"的禪義。三十年彈指過去,其間我藝事每有進境,大體和我在敦煌那段短暫的生涯有着內在的聯繫。歲月秋霜染鬢毛,丹青不知老將至,今爲昌東兄作序,曷勝今昔之嘆。我更期待他年有日,與昌東再聽塞外的鳴沙,回味那少年的夢境。

范曾於甲戌年南開大學北村
(中國當代著名畫家、南開大學教授)

A Rosy Dream Along the Silk Road
Preface to Mr Tang Changdong's Album

Fan Zeng

The hiking tour with my classmates from Xi'an to the Hexi Corridor 30 years ago brought me before a rosy dreamland of the Silk Road, an area stretching far and wide, rich in magnificent Chinese culture. A similar vision was brought back to my mind by Mr Tang's album of facsimiles of mural paintings, over 120 in quantity.

Having been to the capital city of 11 dynasties, Chang'an had virtually developed into a world metropolis by the time of Tang Dynasty, where assembled a galaxy of talents and genius engrossing in literary and artistic pursuits. Meanwhile, thousands of merchants from central and western Asian countries and from as far as Rome converged to do business in Chang'an then, which was comparable to what is taking place in Guangzhou and Shenzhen today. Such a scene of prosperity was attributed to the relative social stability of the society which was the indirect effect due to the construction of the Great Wall by the First Emperor, Qinshihuang. The wall was an effective protection of the greatest agricultural country of the east from the invasion by the non-Han nationalities in the north and west. Stability brought forth the boom of economy. As were the northern minorities blocked outside, so was the birth of the Silk Road. Admittedly, of the works preserved in the tombs, temples and grottoes, some were meant to display the power and dignity of the Han nationality and to even flaunt the luxury and extravagant ease of the nobility, but most were repesentative of the cultural exchanges between China and the countries like India and those in the central and western Asia. As is stated that "The celestial melody accompanied by drumbeats in temples is none but a combination of Chinese and Indian music which slides afar."

Fascinated as he was by the frescos in the Tang tombs around Xi'an. Mr Tang was not confined in this area only: his footprint can be found in the Hexi Corridor, north of the Qilian Mountain in Gansu and further west in the Buddhist grottoes along the Tarim River, including the Mogao, the Yulin, the Kezier, the Kumtula and the Berzikili. Mountains or rivers, wind of dew, have never held back from his pursuits in the past 18 years as long as there are frescos ahead. Facing the walls and warming his hands by breathing onto them in the past, Mr Tang has been totally committed to the task of making facsimiles. As the famous monks Xuan Zang and Jian Zhen were to Buddhism, so is Mr Tang to frescos. Lofty is the word for his utter dedication and piety, his unswerving determination, and his negligence of fame and wealthy, Either the art of religion or the religion of art demands complete dedication "without ever bothering to think about other dreams." The frescos have unfolded before him an amazing realm of art, full of delight and charm. His wish to pubilsh his reproductions to let the public share his delight is unselfishness itself.

Buddhist doctrine says that all reality is a phantom, and all phantoms real. There is neither idol nor Creator, and all starts from nowhere and ends nowhere. All of a sudden, there is everything and anything. This is due to the whimsicality of the universe. Moving from the chaotic reality to the state of nonexistence is the attainment of being a Buddha. If so, why the galzing frescos in the Buddhist temples and grottoes? Isn't this contrary to the doctrine of nonexistence, according to which all forms disappear as the wind blows away the cloud? To me, this contradiction is just the difference between art and philosophy, or rather, art is the stair to philosophy. At the zenith of the Buddhist philosphy, there is no mural painting, nor sculptures but the Buddha's footprint and the bodhi tree.

No matter who were the occupants of the tombs, crown princess or princess, nobles or aristocrats, they all cherished a non-religious understanding of fate. Infatuated with worries and fears at heart, they were reluctant to depart with their luxury without ever pondering over mercy and the Buddhist doctrine that good has its reward and evil its recompense. Whatever the contents of the painting, huntings, reception ceremonies, garden parties, polo-playing, maids, guests of envoys, none was not meant to display the royal power and glory, a nostalgia in nature. But, great were the artists who took the chance to show their talents and express their sympathy for the humble maids and men of strength and courage, just as the maids at a royal wedding were not dancing for the heavenly union but for the love of music. In fact, the frescos dazzle our eyes with the brilliance of a treasury of customs, soical life and dressing styles of the era. Take for example the dress worn by the non-Han maid, what a sharp contrast between that and the costumes of the imperial concubines, and how progressive the painters were in their mentality! This reminds me of Bai Juyi's poetic expression of his indignation:

> The wearers look all the more brilliant,
> And the knitting maids fall deeper into oblivion by each stitch.

The Tang Dynasty lasted about 280 years and can be divided into 4 periods, the first about a century long, a period of peace and repid accumulation of wealth, and the rest can be neatly subdivided into 360-year periods, characterstic of reaching and passing from its zenith and being on the wane. Men of parts and talents emerged in response to the proper time and conditions of the great Tang Dynasty. As Su Dongpo said, "Poetry by Du fu, prose by Han You, calligrahpy by Yan Zhenqing and painting by Wu Daozhi are perfection itself. Everything has its tradition. By the time of the Tang Dynasty, all these artistic pursuits had reached their pinnacles." The elaborate achievement in painting of the Tang times is wonderfully shown by Mr Tang's reproductions. The master painters of the Jin and Tang Dynasties were, as agreed, Gu Kaizhi, Lu Tanwei, Zhang Yanyuan and Wu Daozhi. According to Zhang Yanyuan, "The ingenious brushwork of Gu Kaizhi and Lu Taiwei is not a renewal but a creation of dense strokes, a style of continuous lines which show strength out of gracefulness. Their delicate composition and shaping style seem to be continuation of Wei Xie's style". The style of dense strokes reached its culmination in the hands of Zhou Fang though the brilliant cultivation of Zhang Xuan . The impact of this style can be discerned in the grottoes, and in the works of Weichi Yi, the painter and monk in the Tang Dynasty, coming to the Central China from the remote southwest, whose artistic attainments " are compatible to those of Gu Kaizhi and Lu Tanwei" and were as" high " as those of Yan Liben and Wu Daozhi. The most influential of the Tang painting style was the "sparse strokes", initiated by Zhang Sengyao, a well－known painter in the 5th century and brought about by the "combination of the Han civilization and the non－Han civilization" as Yao Zui commented. Influenced by the bold and unconstrained painting style of the Han Dynasty and the superb techniques introduced from India, Zhang Senyao, with his rare originality, culitivated his own style, a magnificent style to influence Wu Daozhi 200 years later. To borrow Zhang Yanyuan's commentary, "Though slightly dissimilar in talent and wit, Zhang Sengyao and Wu Daozhi are very similar in style. Both are quick-handed and their paintings may even seem lack of strokes here and there, but artistic omissions enrich the appeal and charm all the more ." Wu Daozhi, definitely the master hand of his times, was wielding his brush at a lightning speed, as if ever pushed by his brimming enthusiasm and inspiration. Su Dongpo, a well-noted poet in the Song Dynasty, wrote, " His brush is wielded swiftly like the wind, as if pushed all along by his overwhelming spirit. Alas, it is quick as a shadow follows a candle. All his strokes, now here and then there, vertical, horizontal, or slant, are but harmonious as a whole to an extreme degree, " Wu's bold and vigorous style was commensurate with the cultural spirit of the era. For instance, in calligraphy, there was Zhang Xu who "executes his brush as a tornado moves. " In poetry, there was He Zhizhang who " composes poems at an incredible speed. "In sword－dance, there was Gongsun Daniang who "conducts her sword as suddenly as lightening" Wu Daozhi lived in a colorful age, full of enthusiasm and fervor and his paintings were imbued with the merry mood of the great Tang Dynasty at its heyday. In a word , his style might be summarized as " bold strokes with soft coloring, " a precious heritage for the Song and Yuan painters.

It is fortunate that some of Zhou Fang's paintings are still well-preserved in scrolls, but Zhang Yanyuan's and Wu Daozhi's works of art, mainly mural paintings, suffered a miserable fate, most of which were missing and destroyed in wars, buried underground as the grottoes collapsed, and faded in color and finally disappeared by weathering over the past thousand of years. Anyway, Wu Daozhi had his worshippers and followers in all later dynasties, one of whom was Wu Zongyuan, a Song Dynasty painter. But, most valuable are Mr Tang's reproduction of the Tang frescos and his penetrating insight into the evolution of the "dense strokes " and "sparse strokes ", too artistis styles characteristic of ancient Chinese paintings. He didn't attribute to fortuity the emergence of the greatest master painter Wu Daozhi, and asserted that Wu's style was elaborately shown in the paintings in the tombs of Yongtai, Yide, Zhanghuai and Weihao. The bold and brief lines and the delicate coloring are definitely Wu's influneces. The paintings on the eastside wall of the passage to prince Zhanghuai's tomb are most representative of Wu's execution of coloring and drawing lines, unconstrained, flowing and vigorous. Where there is a mountain there is a peak, just as there is the Taishan Mountain towering over all the others, so was Wu Daozhi, whose emergence was the culmination of the ancient Chinese paintings.

Mr Tang has committed himeslf to the task of studying the techniques of the Tang mural paintings, researching on art history, and copying the frescos in the past two decades, and allowed nothing to deter him or intervene. He has achieved what may be expected the most of such a career. His. reproductions have retained the appeal, beauty and charm of the original. They look like the real both in appearance and spirit. The communication he has with the ancient masters is just like that between bosom friends. The rustle of his brush moving along the paper voices his reverence for them. As the saying goes, " where wholehearted dedication is directed, the whole world will step aside to let you in. " I am really short of words for his dedication and commitment, and for his brilliant reproductions which, I can only say, are exquistite past compare.

30 years ago when I was in my 20s, I took lodgings for some time in a shabby Taoiat temple at the foot of the Sanwei Mountain. When the moon was shining above. I would go out and sit on the slope, in the meditative mood, looking eastward to Chang'an(the prsesent day Xi'an) where there would be people bustling about or westward to the desert and wilderness where stands the Gate of Jade, beyond which" Spring wind never blows. " Night by night the lonely moon was shedding her rays over the silent earth. "The moom is intelligent, " as the Sixth Buddha observed. In the moon light my worries and desires all disappeared and I could somehow understand the Buddhist doctrine that "To be free from worries is to get closer to Sakyamuni. " 30 years has passed as if in an instant, during which, if any progress has been made in my artistic pursuits, it is intrinsically related to the hiking tour along the Silk Road. Gray hairs appear on my temples but an artist will remain unaware of age. All sorts of feelings are welling up in my heart while writing this preface. It is my great anticipation that I will be able to embark on a tour with Mr Tang along the Silk Road to renew my rosy dream.

Professor of Fine Arts,
1994, Nankai University, Tianjin.
(famous modrn artist and professor of Nan Kai University)

序

常沙娜

七十年代初,我偶得機會曾專程去古都長安,臨摹永泰公主墓的部分壁畫,其間認識了陝西省博物館的年輕畫家唐昌東同志,他那種青年人少有的對墓室壁畫的憧憬和臨摹的熱情,給我留下了很深的印象。

如今,二十年已過去,我不時地聽説昌東同志一直堅持着面壁古代壁畫的摹寫和研究的生涯。他立足於唐代,除了墓室的壁畫以外,還深入地展開,沿着絲綢之路的石窟寺壁畫,西至甘肅的敦煌莫高窟和新疆的拜城克孜爾石窟,對唐代壁畫藝術進行了比較系統,且有深度的摹寫研究。

昌東同志之所以能夠長期與唐代壁畫結下不解之緣,是與他的閲歷和扎實的繪畫功底及藝術素養分不開的。他少年時代畢業於湖北藝術學院附中,因成績優秀被保送到西安美術學院國畫系深造,得益於深厚的傳統繪畫基礎。1962 年畢業後,他任職於陝西省博物館,曾爲該館的陳列先後創作了《鄭成功》、《林則徐》、《詩人杜甫》、《文成公主入藏》等優秀的歷史畫。此外,他還創作了毛主席在陝北的《同甘共苦》和朱老總在南泥灣的《屯墾之前》等大幅的革命歷史畫。

七十年代初,古都長安百里境内相繼發掘清理了一批具有重要歷史和藝術價值的唐代墓冢。這些墓室的發掘和所寶藏的壁畫、文物等珍寶轟動了國内的美術、工藝美術、史學等各方面的專家,自然也引起了國外同行專家們的關注。墓室的壁畫規模和内容爲填補和研究中國美術史,唐代人物畫和壁畫藝術提供了極爲重要的真迹和史料,如乾縣的唐永泰公主墓、章懷太子墓、懿德太子墓以及三原的淮安靖王李壽墓室中都極其生動地繪製了與墓室主人身份相應的,反映當時禮儀、服飾風格、生活等精美而寫實的壁畫。對此,做爲具有深厚繪畫功底的昌東同志,面臨如此大量的古代精美壁畫怎能不受到感染,他責無旁貸的投入了這些墓室壁畫的臨摹工作,而且被深深的吸引住了。他與他的同事們憑借着微弱的燈光,忘卻了墓室的陰暗和潮濕,滿懷着對傳統繪畫的激情,品味着古代畫師們的遺迹,學習着先師們的傑作。這些未署名的畫師名作如:永泰墓的"宫女圖"、章懷墓的"觀鳥捕蟬圖"、"馬球圖"、"迎賓圖"、"狩獵出行圖"等作品都不愧與唐代名師閻立本的"步輦圖"、"歷代帝王圖"相媲美。然而這些墓室的壁畫的内容和精美畫面的發掘,因受其環境和條件的限制,很難爲各界人士親臨其境地去體會和了解,更難於中外人士目睹其貌,這就需要以優秀的摹本全面展示,供世人去領會、鑒賞和研究。摹本的真實性與其藝術水平直接關係到原作的真貌,摹寫的繪畫藝術技巧和意義無疑就顯得更爲重要了,這是任何攝影技術所難以替代的。昌東同志就其投入的功夫和其藝術修養及繪畫水平,都達到了能負重任的臨摹水準。

1974 年秋,我國首次在日本專題展出"中國漢唐壁畫展"。當時昌東同志負責臨摹唐代壁畫部分,出國展之前曾在北京預展,我又一次得機會欣賞了他所摹的壁畫,他真切的再現了唐代墓室壁畫的面貌和内在韻味,得到藝術家們的讚賞。此展覽在日本也一舉成功,深得日本美術及史學家們的重視和讚譽,北九州市的美術館館長、日本美術史學家谷口鐵雄先生還專門請昌東同志爲該館復製了《觀鳥捕蟬》、《持扇宫女》等壁畫摹本,收爲該館永久的珍藏。

昌東同志并未滿足當年在摹寫唐墓壁畫所達到的傳神和神似的藝術水平,而是繼續面壁摹寫唐代各類壁畫,更深一步的感悟到原壁畫的綫描、筆墨的運用和著色暈染的層次和内在的韻味,對唐代墓室壁畫和石窟壁畫的藝術風格也做了相應的深入研究和比較。對臨摹的結合也頗爲深刻,正如他在《唐墓壁畫的臨摹》

一文中所闡述的那樣：臨摹要達到較高的藝術境界還是很要點學問的，絕不是像有人所説是不費腦筋的技術勞動，或是依樣畫葫蘆的簡單照抄和模仿，就繪畫技法而論，不論其造型能力、筆墨技巧、賦彩技法都要有對壁畫的深刻的體會理解，駕馭摹寫的同時又要有熟練的技能和對其內容情節的瞭解，并具有較全面的繪畫和文化歷史的素養。摹寫得"像"還不應是表面的"像"，而要刻劃物象的造型、綫條的力度，表達原作內在的神韻才是。昌東同志還聯繫他在摹寫永泰公主墓的"宮女圖"時更加細膩的體會到：墓道的宮女們形象各異，姿容各不相同，人物的性格特徵鮮明，其形象的塑造是以高度概括的綫條表現的，充分發揮了傳統繪畫中"綫"的表現力，宮女們的臉部描繪輕入落筆，筆中圓轉又有輕重的按捺起伏，在微妙的轉折變化中勾畫出富有神態表情的眼、眉、鼻、唇、耳等簡潔的造型，宮女的鬢髮虛出虛入深得毛根出膚之妙，其服飾衣紋綫條渾厚圓潤流暢，主輔分明，疏密濃淡有致，意寫出衣服的飄動和質感，這種嫺熟灑脱的豪邁氣慨與綫描技法的特徵，恰好表現了吳道子的"吳帶當風"的意味和疏體的畫風。

在用墨著色方法上，昌東同志也有其深刻的體會和經驗，提出面對壁畫的各種色彩效果要以總色調爲基礎，再按層次多次暈染或鋪色，一層層加重體現色彩的變化，必要時"畫龍點睛"似地突出部分提神的較亮的顏色，但不能留下塗抹的痕迹，有時壁畫的色彩較薄，但效果卻應顯得濃厚才有"壁"的感覺。造型與筆墨要融爲一體，做到墨有中色，色中有墨的渾然效果，整個畫面的色調要不浮不滯，忌"紅綠的火氣"，想必也是中國傳統繪畫著色最成熟的，稱之爲"渾化"的境界。

唐代壁畫多用礦物質顏料，質地較好，石色不變，用得恰當畫面感覺厚重沉着，但也不宜一遍即用得很厚，也需層層加重，否則畫面會鮮艷得"火氣"浮淺。掌握好賦彩的技法需對傳統色彩的應用、顏料的性能，紙張的特性有較深、熟練的掌握和認識。古代墓室壁畫在地下埋藏了成百年或上千年，經歷了年代的腐蝕風化，整個畫面出現了一種特有的潤澤、沉着、渾厚的基調，呈現出微妙的色彩變化，利用這種變化來進行適當的"處理"。"作舊"也應一遍遍地深入暈染，以達到表現牆面因埋藏多年經泥水浸蝕的朦朧變化效果，或作出部分殘破的泥皮裂紋，適當的殘缺壁畫效果往往也給人以完美的感受和聯想。總之，不論是著色、勾勒或"作舊"都要本着忠實於原作的精神面貌，表現其內在的韻味和題材內容爲準則。

以上的臨摹成果和體會，都是昌東同志經過幾十年的的實踐探索，所達到的得心應手，掌握得微妙微肖的程度。現在能有機會將他面壁二十余年，苦心作畫、研究的成果精選并彙成《大唐壁畫》出版於世，這既是爲弘揚我國傳統繪畫藝術的需要，也是對他幾十年來的成績予以總結和鼓勵，這是他從事古代壁畫臨摹、研究成果的結晶。本書的出版發行將使他如願以嘗的實現他多年地夙願，祝願本書的問世，能爲弘揚祖國傳統藝術，獲得更廣泛的社會效益。

1994 年春節於北京
（中央工藝美術學院院長、教授）

Preface

Chang Shana

My trip to the ancient capital city of Xi′an in the early 1970s which helped me copy the mural Paintings in Princess Yongtai's tomb, gave me the chance of knowing Mr Tang Changdong, then a young painter at the Shaanxi Provincial Museum. His youthfulness and zeal for copying the frescos in the ancient tombs made a lasting impression on me.

In the past 20 years since then, I have heard many a time that though Mr Tang has been totally committed to the task of copying the frescos in the tombs in Shaanxi, in temples and such art treasuries along the Silk Road as the Mogao Grotto in Gansu, and Kezier Grotto in Xinjiang, he has also made researches on the Tang frescos pregnant with brilliant insight, his dedication to such a career is really remarkable.

His indissoluble bond to the frescos is closely related to his rich life experience, excellent mastery of painting skills and artistic accomplishment. Soon after his graduation from the High School Attached to Hubei Academy of Fine Arts , Mr Tang was recommended to study in Xi′an Academy of Fine Arts , where he graduated in 1962 and was assigned to work at Shaanxi Provincial Museum as a painter. Since then he has brought out such exquisite historical paintings for exhibtits there as Zheng Chenggong, Lin Zexu, Poet Du Fu and Princess Wencheng Entering Tibet, and such fine revolutionary paintings as Sharing the Weal and Woe about Chairman Mao Zedong's life in Yanan and Ready to Reclaim the Barren Hills about Commander − in − chief Zhu De in Nanniwan.

In the early '70s, a good deal of Tang tombs, treasuries of art, were successfully excavated 50 miles around the ancient capital city of Xi'an. The mural paintings and historic relics unearthed from the tombs created a furore among painters, artists and historians all over China, and a no less sensation among the artists and experts abroad. The spectacular frescos with their particular contents have provided invaluable first − hand materials for the study of the history of Chinese fine arts, figure painting in the Tang Dynasty, and techniques of mural paintings. Splendid and realistic, the frescos in such tombs as of Princess Yongtai, Crown Prince. Zhanghuai, Crown Prince Yide all excavated in Qianxian County, and Li Shou, Prince of Peace, in Sanyuan County, vividly reflect the positions of the occupants and truly unfold the court etiquette, dressing styles, and life patterns of the time. How could Mr Tang resist the temptation before such a treasury of art since he had already been a painter of superb skllls by then? With no hesitation, he set out to copy them. With his colleagues, Mr Tang was totally committed to the task in the dim light and humidity in the tombs, only warmed up by his great enthusiasm for the works of art by ancient masters. Paintings like Palace Maids in Princess Yongtai's tomb, Watching Bird and Catching Cicada in Crown Prince Zhanghuai's tomb, Playing Polo , Receiving Foreign Guests and Hunting Procession can be favorably compared with Travelling by Carriage, and Portraits of the Kings in History by the great Tang painter Yan Liben. Exquisite as they are, these mural paintings, due to their environment and location, deny the easy access to them for people both at home and abroad to appreciate their unique beauty or even to have a simple look, hence the necessity for bringing them out in imitation to the public and experts alike. Since the authenticity and craftsmanship of the imitations are crucial to the original in appeal and signficance, artistic copying seems all the more outstanding. Photos help little in this field. As for the dedication, the artistic attainments and even the time involved, Mr Tang has done the greatest for this job of unique importance.

Before The Exhibition of Chinese Murals from the Han to Tang Dynasty was held in Japan in 1974, there had been a rehearsal in Bejing to which I attended. The imitations of the Tang frescos were out of Mr Tang's hand. The rehearsal served as a chance for me to appreciate his superb skills of capturing the intrinsic beauty and charm of the original frescos. The Exhibition amazed Japenese audience, of whom, Tetuo Taniguti, curator of the Arts Gallery of Kitakyushu, and a well − known historian, pleaded Mr Tang to reproduce Watching Bird and Catching Cicada, and Palace Maids for preservation in the Gallery. Mr Tang's facsimiles of those years were not merely alike to the original in appearance but also alike in spirit. A point shoud be made here that Mr Tang's great attainments did not serve as achievements with which he could rest content, but as an impetus for him to copy more, and to study harder the line techniques, excecution of colors and the intrinsic charm revealed in the paintings. Moreover, Mr Tang has done remarkable researches on the frescos in the Tang tombs and on those in the grottoes as well, all with brilliant insight. As for the imitaion, He said in his Magnificent Frescos from the Great Tang Dynasty that artistic imitaion involves much leaming, not being something that merely needs skills or is simple mechanical copying. The ability to conceive, the fine shaping of objects and figures and the techniques in brushwork and coloring are none but the results of thorough understanding of the contents and plots of the frescos, and a comprehensive knowledge of the history of culture and drawing. Being alike in appearance is the minimum requirement of making facsimiles and the goal is to capture the intrinsic beauty and charm, the power of the lines and the spirit of the original. According to Mr Tang, Palace Maids is one of the best that represent the highest artistic achievement, "of the maids, each is particular in her appearance, posture, attitude and character, and the creation of the these beautiful maids is mainly done by a subtle use of lines, a technique characterstic of traditional Chinese paintings. The strokes employed in depicting their faces are ligh, graceful and exquisite. The softening and darkening of the lines, alternatively used where necessary, give subtle expression to their inner feelings by their eyes, brows, noses, lips and ears. The combination of decisive and evasive lines in depicting their hair vigorizes the hair as if it had a life of its own. The lines in representing the costumes, distinct and graceful, smooth and continuous, softened here and darkened there, produce the effect of being fluttering and substantial. The power, the grandeur and the techniques of line depiction perfectly represent the style of 'sparce strokes', ardently advocated by the Tang masterpainter Wu Daozhi."

Mr Tang's interpretation of coloring is remarkable, too. He wrote that a base color shoud be determined before the actrual copying, then upon which to apply the dyestuff several times without obvious traces, and even to darken the color sometimes with the view of producing the desired effect. He said: "On the occasion when the colors of the orignial are too thin to bring out the effect of being thick, heavy strokes are called for, and the depiction and coloring must be integrated to such a degree that the facsimiles seem neither ostentatious nor dull, nothing to say being a mass of the red and green colors." I believe that this is the most accurate interpretation of the coloring techniques in traditional Chinese paintings. The colors used in creating the frescos mainly made from natural ores, good in quality and not easy to fade, when properly used, often produce an effcet of being thick. Despite such a property, they should be thinly applied in several times, or, the reproductions will seem too loud. Coloring effect also depends on the quality and properties of the paper in use. The mural paintings having remained underground for over a thousand of years have undergone enough changes, therefore, show a unique mixed tone of briliancy and coolness, hence the necessity of deliberate wearing - off, to make the imitations seem old by patient work of coloring. The wearing - off must effectuate a sense of vagueness and even show crackles of the original due to a long underground life. In fact, artistic flaws often set forth intellectual associations. However, the application of colors, the drawing of lines and the wearing - off must all be faithful in spirit to the original with no other purpose than recapturing the beauty and charm of the original. These are the principles which Mr Tang has followed.

The publication of his Magnificent Frescos from the Great Tang Dynasty along the Silk Road, a crytalizagtion of his wisdom, artistic attainments and industry in the past 20 years, is as much the pinnacle of his achievements as an attempt to spread the art of traditional Chinese painting. More than a personal realization of Mr Tang Changdong's long - cherished wish, the Album will win a wide acclaim and produce a greater social effect. For this, I sincerely wish.

1994, Beijing
(Professor and president to Beijing Academy of industrial Art)

唐墓壁畫的臨摹

唐昌東

中國古代的壁畫藝術,有着兩千多年的悠久歷史,在我們民族的繪畫史上有極其輝煌的成就。它獨特的藝術風格與氣派,在世界文明史上占有很重要的地位。

解放以來,隨着國家對文物事業的重視,考古工作的不斷發展,不僅對遺留地面的石窟寺壁畫進行了維修保護,同時又發掘清理了許多埋藏了幾千年的秦、漢、隋、唐時期的墓室壁畫。這些壁畫墓室尤如一座座地下畫廊,是我們學習祖國傳統藝術,研究古代繪畫的寶貴資料。爲保存珍貴的文物資料,提供向國內人民陳列展出的作品和向世界各友好國家進行文化交流,壁畫的臨摹無疑是一個重要方法和途徑。

早在 40 年代初,爲"窮探六法之根源"六朝隋唐之真迹,"以證史闕",張大千先生就投荒面壁敦煌三年,臨摹了一批北朝至唐、五代各時代的壁畫珍品,當它在成都、重慶、上海展出問世的時候,曾引起國內學術界極大的震動,被"敦煌學"的倡議者陳寅恪先生讚譽爲"敦煌學"領域中不朽的"盛事"。

1974 年 10 月,我國的漢唐壁畫首次在日本展出,并先後巡展美歐,得到國外專家學者極大的關注和重視,向世界各友好國家的人民進行了文化交流。從文物事業來講,臨摹工作應是很重要的一個方面。

———————— 一 ————————

臨摹,任何從事美術事業的人都不陌生,人們在開始接觸繪畫的時候,也常常是從臨摹開始的,即是美院中國畫系的學生,也要經過臨摹階段,具體的學習民族繪畫的傳統技藝、筆墨技法,掌握傳統的創作方法和藝術規律。這種在初階段的臨摹,老師總是要求"老老實實"的將所臨的作品"臨像"。但經過一段時間的寫生練習,學生具備了一定的表現能力以後,再去臨摹作品時,老師又常常要學生不要臨的"太像",臨摹主要是體會原作的精神,加以借鑒,要從別人的作品中跳出來、慢慢創造自己的風格。從學習、繼承祖國的傳統技法的目的來講,這種要求是正確的。

今天我們所談的臨摹和這種以學習借鑒爲目的的臨摹不同,而是保存古代壁畫繪製一件寶貴的文物資料或陳列展品。因而我們的臨摹原則,是要忠於原壁畫客觀的臨摹。即在臨摹中,不保留自己的藝術風格,或是某些喜愛,要求畫面的大小,構圖,每一物象的造型用筆和色彩都要完全忠於原壁的面貌,摹品完成後的效果,基本和原壁一樣,甚至達到"亂真"程度的"酷似"。這種臨得"像"還不是表面的"像"而是要每一刻劃物象的造型、綫描、既不差之毫厘又要每一綫條的力度韻味,都表達出原作的神韻,著色暈染畫到酷似畢肖。自然要再現古代畫師高超的技藝,傳神境界,非僅真似而已。這對即是在美術學院受過良好專業訓練的美術工作者來說,也并非是一件輕易的事。

臨摹是可高可低,可深可淺的事。美院的學生、研究生、專家和教授同樣是臨摹,但他們的素養不同,作品是不能相提并論的。張大千先生所臨的敦煌壁畫,對傳統技巧的研究,在敦煌學領域極大的貢獻,未必是我們能寫點東西可比擬的。他的造型、綫描功力,他對古壁畫迹演變的洞察之深,又有幾個畫家能達到和相比。解放後敦煌老一輩的專家和美院老師所臨的敦煌摹品也頗令人嘆服,像董希文先生所臨的北魏時期的薩捶那太子本生壁畫,色調的沉着典雅、造型的生動傳神,都給我留下了極深的印象。我想正是他們有深厚的繪畫功力和全面修養,摹品才能畫得深切感人,超乎神境。畫畫在某種程度是畫自己的藝術素養和感受。臨摹要達到較高的藝術境界,那還是很要點學問的。絕不是像有的人所說:"不費腦筋的技術勞動"或是"依樣畫葫蘆的簡單的照抄和模仿"。就繪畫技術而論,不論其造型能力、筆墨技巧、賦彩技法,其每一方面都有很深的學問,要駕馭它同時又需要熟練的技能,對從事文物工作的臨摹者來說,必須具備一定的專業基礎和較全面的繪畫素養。

繪畫是通過可視的物象來表現客觀現實的。在繪畫中首先接觸的就是造型問題。顧愷之提出的"以形寫神"，六法中的"應物象形"，都無不是談到造型問題。造型能力對從事臨摹工作的同志來講，也是首先要解決的基本功之一。學點素描是必要的，這能很好的培養造型能力，訓練從繪畫角度整體的去觀察對象，準確地把握對象的輪廓比例、特征及明暗層次變化等等。實踐中逐步認識畫面中哪些東西是主要的應該強調，哪些是次要的應該減弱，克服瑣碎描繪對象及"謹毛而失貌"(劉安《淮南子》)的毛病，學會概括整體表現物象的本領。只有能準確的刻劃形象，才能領悟神依形而在，掌握傳神的奧秘。

　　當然，即使具備了很強造型能力的人，是并不一定就能完成一幅好的中國畫白描的。更談不上就能畫出綫形的神韻。我們的民族繪畫不像西洋畫中寫實的具象描繪，又不是現代西方抽象藝術流派的不似表現，它是以意象的表現形式而獨立於世界藝術之林。中國畫的綫描不同於西洋畫中塑造形體結構的輪廓綫，而是塑造形體的用筆即綫描本身就有着獨立的美學價值。傳統繪畫強調"骨法用筆"，不論是剛健挺拔，遒勁灑脱或渾厚圓潤，在運筆中表現的輕重、徐疾、轉折、頓挫等不同的變化，又都和飽含内在精神的情感，融爲一體，表達出物象之神韻。"夫象物必在於形似，形似須全其骨氣，骨氣形似，皆本於立意而歸乎用筆"。(張彦遠《歷代名畫記》)，對表現物象"形似"用筆的重要及内發心源的立意關係張彦遠是講得深入淺出，極爲透徹的。我們民族繪畫歷來講"外師造化、中得心源"，用筆亦在"外肇造化，内發心源"，方能迹呈"婉曲之妙"。學好中國畫"骨法用筆"是不能等閑視之的。在用筆方面古代畫師們有很高的造詣。張彦遠曾論述吳道子作畫"或自臂起，或從足先"都能"膚脈連結"，"彎弧挺刃，植柱構梁，不假直尺"。蘇軾也曾説："道子畫人物，如以燈取影……得自然之數，不差毫末"。我們的摹品要再現古代畫師們精湛的技藝，爲之傳神，倘没有很好的造型基礎和綫描功力，那將是無能爲力的。

　　對於色彩的認識，從臨摹來看掌握傳統的方法是必須的。但僅此卻又遠遠不夠，因我們所臨的壁畫，年代久遠，畫面色彩發生了復雜的變化，即是原來礦物質的石色，如石青、石綠、朱砂等剝落後亦都發生了異變，每一種顔色都顯得非常豐富，畫面中原是空白的牆面，也有一種朦朧微妙的神妙色調之感。我們就需要吸收西畫中關於色彩的科學原理及不要孤立去看一種顔色的觀察方法，以及色彩冷暖的變化等有益的滋養，使傳統的賦彩方法更加豐富起來。

<h1 style="text-align:center">二</h1>

　　按臨摹製作的一般程序：第一步是描稿。爲了準確的傳達原壁的精神，在情況允許的條件下，一般用透明度很強的滌綸紙(不宜變形)一類的材料，將原壁畫面的輪廓結構，用毛筆按原壁綫條的用筆，粗細變化描畫下來，用古人的説法就是"拓下來"。如不是用綫條表現的地方，有的建築或没骨法表現的地方，則用較細的墨綫的把輪廓描下來(這裏"情況允許的條件"：是指原壁牆面較結實的畫面，但在用膠帶紙時也要注意不能損壞原壁畫面，需貼在畫外牢固的牆面上)。像原壁風化嚴重，容易剝落的地方，最好用幻燈放稿或照像放大的辦法了。對模糊不清的地方，還要對原壁仔細辨認，用鉛筆起稿，以寫生的辦法將模糊不清的畫面強調出來使人看到畫的是什麼内容。值得注意的是不論是拓稿、放稿還是寫生畫稿，都不能簡單從事，必須認真對待。否則，在下一步畫正稿時即使你有很高的造型水平、綫描功力，那也將不能準確無誤，傳達原壁精神。要知道國畫人物，"差之毫厘，便失之千里"是一點也不誇張的。我們在拓稿或起稿以後，還需仔細對原壁將畫稿檢查一遍，修正畫稿中不夠準確的地方。

　　畫正稿，在傳統繪畫中，常稱這叫"落墨"。按所臨畫面的用筆，綫描的濃淡將全部畫面勾勒出來，完成"白描"正稿。臨摹中畫正稿"白描"是極其重要的，也常常是摹品成敗的關鍵。在動筆畫正稿之前，好好體會原壁畫面的意圖，研究作品時代藝術風格的特徵是必要的。但在整個臨摹的程序中，還要更具體地去認識和研究，如畫正稿，就要研究具體的用筆即綫描技法，領悟起筆、運筆、抑揚頓挫等用筆的規律，做到"胸有成竹"，落筆才能大膽肯定，一氣寫成。即是一點一捺，都表現出神完氣足的韻律。不能邊看邊描，筆不貫氣，綫條也會軟弱無力，不僅很難畫出原壁綫描的力度，更難表現綫條的韻味。

　　繪畫發展至唐，六法具備。這一時期的作品；多具有高度的藝術水平，像永泰公主墓的宮女圖及墓道的圉人壁畫形象，章懷太子墓的《觀鳥捕蟬圖》及《禮賓圖》中的人物形象，不但姿容各不相同，人物的性格，特徵鮮明突出"如燈取影"。這些深刻形象的塑造，是用高度概括的綫條表現的。傳統繪畫中的綫描擔負造型任務,它不同於西洋畫取對象明暗調子的描寫方法。而是以綫爲重要的藝術表現手段,對象的結構、空間、質感,都借助於綫的應用。不論人物鞍馬,還是樹木山石、花鳥草蟲,多用中鋒,根據不同的對象,運筆各異,常常是一揮而就,綫條灑脱流暢,又有轉折頓挫,富有韻律,充分地發揮了傳統繪畫中"綫"的表現力。

如唐墓中的宮女形象,臉部描繪輕入落筆,在運筆中既圓轉又有輕重的按捺起伏,在微妙的轉折變化中,一筆成形,畫出眼、鼻、嘴、耳的結構輪廓。宮女的鬢髮虚出虚入、深得"毛根出肉"之妙,壁畫中的服飾衣紋,綫型渾厚圓潤,主輔分明,有粗細疏密的變化,又有一波三折的韻味美感,筆意圓轉起伏,意寫出衣服的飄動和質感。這種灑脱的豪邁氣概,綫描的技法及用筆特徵,明顯地表現了吴道子"蘭葉描"的意味和疏體畫風。我們只有充分的研究和認識了這些原壁的精神,下筆才能"心隨筆運,取象不惑"(荆浩《筆法記》)。傳達原壁内在的精神。如果只作表面的勾勒模仿,是不可能達到超乎神境的藝術高度的。在畫"白描"正稿時,對綫描的濃淡虚實等微妙變化也要注意表現出來。在下一步著色與作舊中,才能非常自然的體現畫面的深度和層次。如畫完後再來提綫,那就因墨色太新,破壞了畫面統一的古壁之感。

壁畫的著色與作舊:在完成正稿的"白描"以後,首先在需要用墨渲染打底子的部分,用不同的墨色即焦、重、濃、淡、輕,根據摹品的需要,用墨染出畫面的濃淡變化,染好染足。傳統的繪畫,講筆以立其形、質,而墨分其陰陽,没有墨便無法表現對象"肉"。所以凡是需用墨暈染的地方,一定要用墨暈染夠,再上顏色。墨色染的不夠,則上色之後畫面就顯得單薄而不沉着,畫面没有份量。用墨暈染時,要注意一遍一遍的上,不宜一遍就想把墨畫夠,否則畫面層次表現不出來,墨色板滯不活。但墨色的暈染也要適可而止,古人曾講"用墨太多,則失其真體,損其筆,而且冗濁"。用墨不可多到掩没了對象形體的程度。

上色和用墨在方法上是相同的。也要多次暈染,一層層的加重,多次暈染,要在畫面上看不到色彩塗抹的痕跡,雖然色彩并不深重,但效果卻顯得濃厚,色彩和負擔着造型任務的筆墨融合一起,墨中有色,色中有墨,整個畫面的色彩,不浮不滯無"紅綠的火氣",這就是中國畫上色最成熟的稱之爲"渾化"的最高境界。暈染一般應畫夠分量即乾後達到原壁畫面效果爲止。但有一點值得注意,對原壁色彩鮮艷和響亮的地方,開始著色時就要保持它的鮮明度,否則就容易畫面完成後色彩效果將比原壁還陳舊灰暗。唐代的壁畫,顏料中的礦物質顏色、質地較好,石色不易變色,用得好畫面感覺厚重沉着。石色覆蓋力較强,要用乳鉢磨細。用時再加桃膠。上石色之前還需用植物色打好底色。石色也不能一遍用得很厚,也要一層層的加。有經驗的畫師在上石色以後還要加上一遍礬水,乾後再罩石色時,第一遍塗的石色就不會被洗掉或是上不均勻。有的石色用的過了,畫面鮮得"火氣",也可以用類似的植物色在上面再罩一遍。總的要完成賦彩這一步,也要我們對傳統色彩的應用、顏料的性能等有較深的認識和研究瞭解。當前許多礦物質顏料都是調配而成的錫管,用此作畫就很難表現古代壁畫色彩的鮮艷、沉着和響亮。應當强調,我們所臨的原壁,因在地下埋藏了多年,歷經久遠年代的腐化風蝕,整個畫面呈現出一種潤澤、沉着、統一和諧的基調。但每一墓室的畫面,也有着不同的微妙的色調變化,不盡相同,即是石窟寺壁畫也不例外。所以臨摹古壁和復製絹本或紙本的古畫不同,它的底色不是簡單的刷一兩遍茶水之類的顏色所能完成的。其實我們開始著色時就包含着"作舊"。因在著色的始終我們都在刻劃古壁色彩的各種變化。在著色前亦可以根據原壁的基調淡淡的刷一層底色,它必須和上色一樣,根據整個畫面的著色同步的一遍一遍的深入,一次一次地用不同的水色去暈染,才能表現出牆面埋藏了多年經泥水浸蝕的朦朧效果,畫出古壁的味道來。對殘破的泥皮裂紋等,同樣亦只能用寫生的辦法,畫出其空間,層次和虚實、質感等。這自然也要一定的繪畫技能,方能深入而不繁瑣,毫無雕琢之痕,雖用白粉卻不顯其"匠氣"。對表現殘破的泥皮用廣告色可以畫出泥土的質感,但畫面的底色如用廣告色,則難免顯得不夠沉着或粉氣,一般還是用國畫色暈染,宜於畫出沉着的韻味。

總之,不論著色和作舊,都應本着忠實於原作的精神爲準則,至於方法都不是絶對和一成不變的,隨着時代的前進,我們在不斷的實踐中臨摹的技巧也一定會有所發展和前進。

Reproduction of the Mural Paintings in the Tang Tombs

Tang Changdong

The mural painting, one of the ancient Chinese artistic forms, well‑noted for its long history of over 2000 years, occupies a brilliant chapter with its distinction and superb skills in the Chinese painting history, and plays an important part in the history of world civilization.

With the development of archaeology and thanks to the attention attached to the preservation of cultural relics since the liberation, not only have frescos in the grottoes and temples on the ground been well mintained, but also have those buried for over a thousand of years in the tombs of the Qin, Han, Sui and Tang Dynaties been successfully excavated. Artistically, these tombs are underground art galleries, providing sufficient firsthand material for the study of ancient Chinese art. To preserve the relics and to display exhibits for people at home and abroad as a means to promote cultural exchanges, reproduction of the frescos is an important way and plays a unique role.

Making imitations of mural paintings is not something new. In the early 1940s, Mr Zhang Daqian, a prominent painter, spent 3 years in Dunhuang copying the precious frescos dated from the period of the Nothern States down to that of the Five Dynasties, with the intention of tracing the " origin of the six artistic styles" , " showing the artistic attainments of the period as a testimony to historical records." The exhibition of his reproductons then in Chengdu, Chongqing and Shanghai created a real sensation in the art circles , and was highly praised as "a spectacular event " by Mr Chen Yinge, a well‑known warm advocator of "Dunhuang Fresco Studies."

In October, 1974, The Exhibition of Chinese Murals from the Han to Tang Dynasty first held in Japan and later in America and Europe, won an international acclaim. It did its part in cultural exchange. Reproduction of the frescos by imitation is indispensable in the preservation of cultural relics.

1

Copying is familiarity to all who take painting as a prefession. In fact, amateur, or professional, one begins his drawing by imitation. As a rule, painting majors take first step of academic training by copying, they must familiarize themselves with the traditional techniques, the brushwork, color application skills, the creative methods and artistic laws. At the beginning students are often asked to make faithful imitations and the highest principle at this stage is to be "honest" and "alike". After some acquisition of the basic techniques to express themselves, they are encouraged by their teachers to make imitation not too "faithful ", and the focus is to capture the spirit of the original in order to cultivate their own styles. This is scientific as far as the heritage of the Chinese painting techniques are concerned.

The copying to be dicussed here, different from that in the classroom, is the compensatory way to show the audience what the original look like. Different purposes demand different disposals. The principle here requires that all imitations be true to the original in size, brushwork and coloring without any sign of the imitators' own sytles, and that the beauty and charm of the original be well recaptured. Anyway, identity in appearance is not all. Every stroke must be as powerful and revealing as the original. What is required here is to make the reproductions alike both in appearance and spirit. This is no easy task even for an artist with an excellent academic training.

Imitations can either be works of art or trash, dependent on one's artistic attainments. Students, experts and professors all make copyings but their works are not compatible. The reproductions by Mr Zhang Daqia, a huge contribution to Dunhuang Fresco Studies, have shown his utmost talents in shaping the objects and figures, in line depiction and his insight into the evolution of the ancient mural paintings. His achievements have never been exeeeded. Since the liberation, generations of painters have been copying frescos in Dunhuang and produced a good deal of works of art. For instance, Mr Dong Xiwen's reproduction of the fresco of Crown Prince Saduona of the Northern Wei period has impressed me a lot with its graceful coloring and dazzling splendor. The fascinating charm and appeal of the copyings depend on nothing but the producer's superb techiques. In a sense, to draw a picture is to draw one's artistic perception and understanding. To make an imitation artistic involves much learning, never being something, as some people argue, that merely needs skills and is simple mechanical imitation. As far as the ability to conceive, brushwork and coloring are concerned, it is as complicated and challenging as anything else. Skills are defintely needed but a competent copier must be one who has an excellent academic training and splendid craftsmanship.

Painting is an art of reflecting reality through visible objects. What arises first is the question of composition (shaping). The idea of "expressing spirit by drawing forms " as advocated by Gu Kaizhi already touched the question of composition ability, one of the basic requirements for a copier. This ability can be fostered through sketching, which requires close observations of the objects and a good mastery of the proportions, characteristics of the objects, and even variations in brightness. Gradually one will get to know what to be stressed and what to be overlooked so as to avoid "over－stressing the trivial at the expence of the more singificant." The ability to depict the object accurately as a whole ensures a subtle expression of the spirit embodied in the image.

It goes without saying that merely good composition competence doesn't guarantee success of a work of art by line drawing, not to mention an exquisite representation of the beauty and charm of the lines. Chinese paintings, like neither the conventional western portrayals nor modern western abstract paintings, occupy in the world art arena a place of its own with its distinction of emphasizing the artistic conception of the images. The lines in Chinese drawings, unlike those used in western paintings for shaping the objects, have a unique aesthetic value in themselves. As bones are to a body, so lines are to traditional paintings. They can be soft, smooth or bold and vigorous and can be light, quick or slow, but they must be expressive in revealing the intrinsic spirit the object possesses. " Paintings must look like the real in form and being alike entirely depends on the spirit they reveal. And to capture the spirit, which is conceived beforehand, relies solely on fine brushowork" (Zhang Yanyuan, An album of Well－known Paintings). What is to express in drawing is conceived in advance and what is expressed is realised by drawing itself. The combination of fine external brushwork and the internal spirit is the highest goal all traditional painters aspire to reach. In fact, many ancient painters were masters in brushwork. As Zhan Yanyuan said, Wu Daozhi "can start a darwing either with the arm or the foot and the portrayal when completed is not inharmonic, with all the lines, curves and straight ones alike, being where they should be." Su Dongpo exclaimed in appreciation that Wu Daozhi drew as swiftly as "a shadow follows a candle and the portrayal seems natural, realistic and harmonious as a whole to an incredible degree."Without the ability to conceive and the talent to draw lines, we can never represent the consummate artistry of the ancient masters through our reproductions. That is certainty.

As for the application of color, traditional methods are necessary but need some improvement, for the mural paintings have undergone sufficient changes, particularly in colors, through a long course of time. The colors, even though made from natrual ores, have changed a lot and got unique effects. Even the blank spaces, vague and obscure now, seem mysterious and beautiful. For this reason, we shouldn't adhere to the principle of observing the single color and trying to represent accordingly, but rather, absorb the western scientific way to combine the warm and cool colors, thus enriching our traditional methods of color application.

2

The first procedure of producing a facsimile is to sketch by tracing, that is , if the condition permits, to glue a sheet of strong paper onto the original with adhensive tapes, and then trace the outlines with a writing brush, just like making a rubbing as the ancient people called (Condition here refers to that of the mural painting which is not easy to peel off, and the tape must be glued where it is strong enough and not liable to damage). If the condition denies, photos or slides are suggested. As for the obscure places, fill them up with what must have been there after a close observation. Great attention is called for whenever it is to make a rubbing, to take a photo or to fill up the blanks with a pencil, otherwise, the next procedure will be extremely difficult if you try to capture the appeal and spirit of the original even if you are talented and well trained. The dictum that an error, the breadth of a single hair , may lead you a thousand li astray, is no exaggeration in making such imitations. After completing the rubbing, close comparison is needed and correction must be made if necessary.

The second procedure, line－drawing the entire picture on the sketch or rubbing, is a key step that determines success or failure of a facsimile. Necessary studies must be made of the intention of the original painter, the artistic styles of the time and the particular line techniques used in the original. Not untill a complete picture is formed up in your mind are you encouraged to start, for confidence is that which guarantees the continuity of drawing the lines, precisely in thickness and width, and letup spoils all. The worst is drawing little by little while looking up again and again.

By the Tang Dynasty, painting had developed into a natural art and most works of the era reached a very high artistic level. Take for example, Palace Maids, and The Waitingman in Princess Yongtai's tomb, Watching Bird and Catching Cicada, and Receiving Foreign Guests in Crown Prince Zhanghuai's tomb, were all vividly presented in their appearance, character and position. What is more significant about them is that all the images were created by lines instead of by the softening and darkening of colors as are common in Western paintings. Lines in Chinese paintings are of a unique importance, for the forms, structures, the blanks and even the sense of depth of the objects whether they are human beings, horses, birds, insects or trees, grass, stone or flower, are all presented by the ingenious use of lines, which can be straight, curving, smooth or bold, just like a melody in lines. Rich variation of the drawing of the lines can be discerned in the creation of these images. The strokes employed in depicting the maids' faces are light and graceful while the delicate distribution of strength in the course of lines, softened here and darkened there, gives a subtle expression to their inner feelings by their eyes, brows, noses, lips and ears. The combination of decisive and evasive lines in depicting their hair vigorizes the hair as if it had a life of its own. The lines in presenting their costumes, distinct, graceful, smooth and continuous, heavy or light, thick or thin, produce the effect of being fluttering and substantial. The power, grandeur and the techniques of line depiction, whether bold and decisive or smooth and light, is something similar to Wu Daozhi's style of sparce strikes. No successful facsimiles could be produced without a thorough understanding of the spirit and style of the original. Superficial similarity is the lowest requirement, far from being artistic, nothing to say great. When line − drawing the picture, great caution should be tended to the subtle softening and darkening of colors in accordance with the original, so as to help produce the effect of depth in the next procedures, otherwise, the freshness of the colors of the lines after the reproduction is completed, will spoil the total effect of being antique.

The tinction and wearing − off can be regarded as the final procedure. Applying ink where needed whith an equal density to that of the original is the first step now. Ink tinction with its variation in density is needed, because without it a painting will be lack depth. Ink, therefore, must be sufficient, or the imitation after coloring may seem dull. Care should be taken that ink tinction is done in several times and to a subtle degree that it is sufficient but without obsucring the image.

This is true of color application, which must be done in several times and little by little to make it as if only one layer of color is coated. All colors must be well blended with the ink so there is ink in them and them in the ink. Never make the facsimile "a mass of red and green" but an integrated piece of colors. harmonious and artistic, the highest requirement of tinction craftsmanship in traditional Chinese paintings. Where it is brilliant in the original must be brilliantly colored each time on your imitation, otherwise, your facsimile when finished may seem darker than the original. The dyes used in the Tang mural paitings were made from natural ores. Generally speaking they are good in quality and not easy to fade. Similar colors are suggested for reproductions after they are ground into powder and mixed with glue. Before the mineral colors are applied, colors made fro plants are often used as a base color. The first layer of mineral colors mustn't be very thick, on which the experienced artist often brushes some vitriol water to prevent uneveness. In case more mineral dyes are used than needed a layer of plant colors should be used to offset. In a word, without a thorough knowledge of the qualities of the colors and the traditional techniques, the procedure of tinction will be extremely difficult. The mineral colors on sale now are ready − made but not to our purpose. Since the mural paintings having remained underground for many centruies have undergone enough changes, thus show a unique mixed tone of brilliancy and coolness, looking heavy but not dull, glazing but not loud. Frescos remaining under different connditions have different changes in colors and brightness, different techniques are called for imitations of paintings on different materials. Tea is all right for the base color for reproductlons of paintings on silk scrolls or paper, but can not do for fresco reproduction. The latter is a meticulous work. Its tinction goes step by step with wearing − off, therefore, great care must be taken during the coures of color application to produce the exact color effect of the orignal. Deliberate wearing − off, to show the antique sense of the orignal in reproductions, can be achieved only by patient work of coloring. Crackles are found in many frescos and can be reproduced first by pencil shetching and then tincted by poster colors to show the unique sense of the unique antique wall. Anyway, Poster colors are not appropriate for base colors, for they are too brilliant. High techniques are required for the reproduction of mural paintings but too much craftsmanship will show just the opposite.

In a word, as for color application or deliberate wearing − off, faithfulness in spirit to the original in the highest principle to be observed throughout the complete course of the imitation, methods never remian absolute. New ways will be surely found in the practice of mural painting copying.

圖版目錄 CONTENTS

長安 固原墓室壁畫
FRESCOES FROM THE TOMBS
IN CHANGAN AND GUYUAN

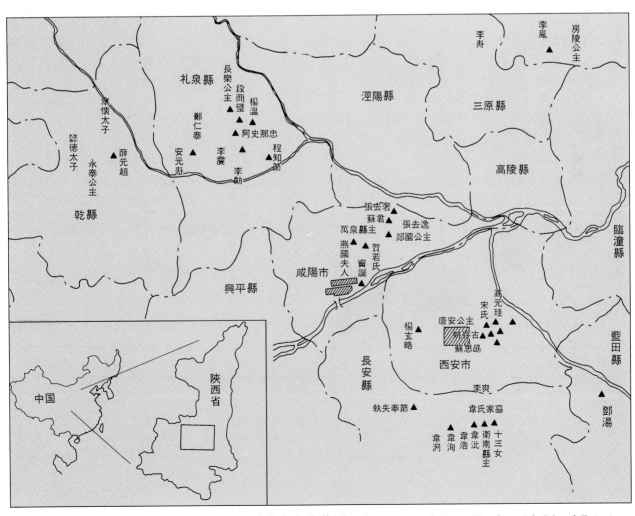

陝西省壁畫唐墓分佈圖 The Layout of Tang Tombs with Mural Paintings

《大唐壁畫》有關唐墓一覽表

Detailed Outline for the Tang Tomb Mural Paintings of Magnificent Frescos from the Great Tang Dynasty

	墓主	身份	生卒年	埋葬年	發掘年	所在地
1	房陵公主	房陵公主	619～673	673	1975	陝西省富平縣
2	李壽	司空公上柱國淮安靖王	577～630	631	1973	陝西省三原縣
3	執失奉節	常樂府果毅、突厥人,執失思力之子	？～658	658	1957	陝西省長安縣
4	李震	梓州刺史	617～665	665	1974	陝西省禮泉縣
5	李爽	銀青光祿大夫守司刑太常伯	593～668	668	1956	陝西省西安市南郊
6	李勣	司空上柱國曹國公右武侯大將軍	594～669	670	1974	陝西省禮泉縣
7	李仙蕙	永泰公主	685～701	706	1960	陝西省乾縣
8	李賢	章懷太子	655～684	711	1971	陝西省乾縣
9	李重潤	懿德太子	683～701	706	1971	陝西省乾縣
10	韋泂	衛尉卿并州大都督	677～692	708	1959	陝西省長安縣南里王村
11	韋浩	武陵郡王	674～692	708	1987	陝西省長安縣南里王村
12	薛氏	萬泉縣主	687～710	710	1953	陝西省咸陽市底張灣
13	張去逸	銀青光祿大夫太僕卿上柱國	692～748	748	1953	陝西省咸陽市底張灣
14	慶山寺遺址			741(建造年)	1985	陝西省臨潼縣新豐
15	蘇思勗	銀青光祿大夫、行內侍省內侍員外	671～745	745	1952	陝西省西安市東郊
16	韋氏家族	(南里王村唐墓)	8世紀	8世紀	1987	陝西省長安縣南里王村
17	唐安公主	唐安公主	761～784	784	1989	陝西省西安市東郊

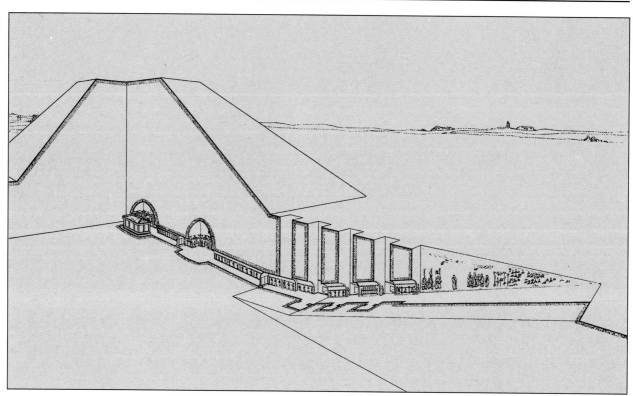

唐墓壁畫位置示意圖(章懷太子墓)
The Location and Illustration of the Tang Tomb Mural Paintings(Prince Zhang Huai's Tomb)

房陵公主墓 Princess Fangling's Tomb

房陵公主是唐高祖李淵第六女。唐咸亨四年(673年)薨,陪葬獻陵。此墓位於陝西省富平縣呂村鄉,1975年發掘。墓由墓道、過洞、天井、甬道、墓室及小龕六部分組成,全長57.8米。墓內壁畫大多殘缺,僅存侍女畫27幅,人物形象高大,綫條奔放,色調高雅。

Princess Fang Ling was the sixth daughter of Emperor Gao Zu(named Li Yuan). She passed away in the 4th year (673 A.D.). After her death she was buried in an attendant tomb near Xianling Mausoleum. The tomb excavated in 1975 is located in Lucun Commune, Fuping County, Shaanxi Province. It is composed of a passageway, a corridor, an air-shaft, a tunnel, a chamber and a small-sized niche with a total length of 57.8 meters. Most of the mural paintings are fragmentary and only 27 pieces remain in good condition. The figures in the paintings are tall and plump and magnanimous and expressive. The paintings are all skillfully created, ingenuously conceived and vigorously lined.

1. 執拂塵侍女 Maidservant Holding a Duster

2. 提壺持杯侍女
Maidservant with Cup and Pitcher

3. 端菓盤待女
Maidservant Carrying a Fruit Tray

李壽墓 Li Shou's Tomb

　　李壽,字神通,唐高祖李淵從弟,官階開府義同三司、上柱國、淮安靖王。唐貞觀四年(630年)薨,加封司空。此墓位於陝西省三原縣陵前公社,1973年發掘。墓爲不規則的圓錐形,有墓道、過洞、天井、小龕、甬道、墓室幾部分,全長44.4米。墓道東、西兩壁以紅帶隔爲上下兩層,上繪對稱的飛天、狩獵,下繪氣勢博大的騎馬出行。過洞、天井、甬道及墓室分別繪步行儀仗、列戟、莊園晨耕、牧養、雜役、重樓建築及庭院、樂舞等壁畫,內容廣泛,題材多樣,真實地記錄了初唐時的社會狀況。

　　Li Shou, also named Sheng Tong, the cousin of Emperor Gao Zu Li Yuan, gained a post of the highest meritorious officer in the rank of the Minister of Public Affairs, the Highest Meritorious Military Officer and was made King of Huai'an when the Tang Dynasty was founded. After his death, he was granted the title "Si Kong", the Minister of Public Affairs. Located in Lingqian Commune, Sanyuan County of Shaanxi Province. the tomb was excavated in 1973. The tomb is in shape of an irregular taper. It is composed of a passageway, a corridor, an air–shaft, a tunnel and a chamber. The tomb with a total length of 44.4 meters, is divided into the east room and the west room whose walls are separated by a red strip, namely the upper part and the lower part. On the upper part of the walls are painted with apsarasand hunting in symmetry. On the lower part of the walls are painted a fresco entitled Riding on Horse Back for an Expedition. On the walls of the passageway, corridor, air–shaft, tunnel and chamber, there are paintings of the Guard of honor in Procession, Display of Halberds, Morning Ploughing in Fields, Herding, Architectures in Palace Style and Courtyard, Music and Dancing etc. These paintings are of broad contents and various subject matters, which reflect the social conditions of the early Tang Dynasty.

4. 狩獵 Hunting

5. 騎馬侍衛 The Imperial Guards on Horse Back

6. 整裝待行 Ready and Wait to Start Out

7. 樂舞 Music and Dance

執失奉節墓 Zhishi Fengjie's Tomb

　　執失奉節,常樂府果毅,突厥人,執失思力之子。唐顯慶三年(658年)卒。此墓位於陝西省長安縣郭杜鎮,1959年發掘。墓道壁畫全部脱落,僅墓室北壁留存舞女(巾舞)圖一幅。

　　Zhishi Fengjie, a Turk, the son of Zhishi Sili held a post in the Imperial Conservatory in the Tang Dynasty. He died in the 3rd year of Xianqing (658 A. D.). Located in Guodu Village, Changan County, Shaanxi Province, the tomb was unearthed in 1959. The mural paintings on the walls of the corridor have completely peeled off, and only one remainder named Dancing Girl exists on the north wall of the chamber .

8. 巾舞 Shawl Dance

李震墓 Li Zhen's Tomb

李震爲李勣長子,官至梓州刺史。唐麟德二年(665年)卒,先其父附昭陵。該墓位於陝西省禮泉縣李勣墓左側,1974年發掘。墓呈圓錐形,墓內壁畫除牛車出行和幾幅侍女外,其它均剝落無存。

Li Zhen, the eldest son of Li Ji, was appointed to be the Governor of Guan Zi District. He died in the 2nd year of Linde (665A.D.) before his father and was buried in Zhaoling Mausoleum. The tomb was on the left side of Li Ji's tomb in Liquan County, Shaanxi Province. Discovered and excavated in the year of 1974, the tomb is in shape of an irregular taper. Unfortunately, all the paintings have fallen off except for Ox Cart on its top and several Waiting Girls.

9. 戲鴨 Playing with a Duck

李爽墓 Li Shuang's Tomb

　　李爽字乾佑,京兆長安人,官至銀青光祿大夫守司刑太常伯。卒於唐總章元年(668 年),與妻鄭氏合葬。李爽墓位於陝西省西安市雁塔區羊頭鎮,1956 年發掘。墓全長 24.5 米,墓道上有三個天井,墓室近於方形。壁畫殘存 25 幅,較完整的有神情動態各異的男女侍 16 幅,每幅間繪梁柱斗拱。

　　Li Shuang, alias Qian You, was a native of the ancientChang'an, capital of the Tang Dynasty, and now Xian instead. He wasthe Post Advisory, Official with a Silver Seal and a Blue Ribbon, performing as the Minister of Memorial Ceremony in charge ofcriminal cases. He died in the first year of the reign of ZongZhang (668 A.D.) and was buried together with his wife nee Zheng inthe grave. Li Shuang's tomb with a total length of 24.5 meters issituated in Yangtou Town, Yanta District Xi'an, Shaanxi Province andunearthed in 1956. There are three air-shafts in the passageway. The chamber is in shape of rectangular, and 25 pieces of paintingsfestooned on the walls, among them only 16 paintings focused onwaiting men and waiting maids with various expressions. They areseparated by columns and Dougongs(a system of brackets insertedbetween the top of a column and a crossbeam).

　　　　　　　　　　　　10. 托盞盤侍女 A Maidservant Carrying a Tray

11. 吹笛樂伎 Maidservant Playing the Flute

李勣墓 Li Ji's Tomb

　　李勣是唐太宗時名將,本姓徐,名世勣,字懋功,隋末瓦崗農民起義創始人之一,歸唐後賜姓李,因避太宗諱改名爲李勣。授司空上柱國,曹國公,右武候大將軍等職。唐總章二年(669年)病亡,陪葬昭陵。此墓位於陝西省禮泉縣,1974年發掘。因墓內潮濕,壁畫殘留樂舞圖一組。

　　Known as Xu Shijie, Li Ji, alias Maogong, was a famous general of Emperor Taizong in the Tang Dynasty. As one of the founders of the Wagang Peasants Uprising at the end of Sui Dynasty, he was conferred the surname Li. In order to avoid using the same word in the given name of Taizong he adopted the single word given name Ji when the Tang Dynasty was founded. He was granted the post of the Highest Meritorious Military Officer, the Military General on the right wing. He met with his death in the 2nd year of the reign Zong Zhang and was buried adjacent to Emperor Tai Zong's Mausoleum. Excavated in the year of 1974, the tomb is situated in Liquan County, Shaanxi Province. It is so wet in the tomb that only one of a series of mural paintings of Music and Dance is preserved.

12. 舞伎 A Dancing Maid

永泰公主墓 Princess Yongtai᾿s Tomb

　　永泰公主名仙蕙, 字穠輝, 是高宗李治與武則天的孫女, 中宗李顯第七女。唐大足元年(701年)被武則天處死, 神龍二年(706年)追封爲永泰公主, 與駙馬武延基一同由洛陽遷葬乾陵陪葬。此墓位於陝西省乾縣, 1960年發掘。墓園有圍牆, 墓由墓道、過洞、天井、小龕、甬道、前後墓室組成, 全長87.5米、寬3.9米、深16.7米, 由墓道到墓室分別繪武士、青龍、白虎、闕樓、儀仗、列戟、平綦圖案、雲鶴及男侍、宮女等, 特別是前室東壁所繪的兩組宮女, 形象優美, 神彩動人, 技巧嫻熟, 綫條流暢瀟灑, 是唐墓壁畫中的珍品。

　　Princess Yong Tai, alias Xian Hui and also Jia Hui, was the granddaughter of Li Zhi, Emperor Gao Zong and Empress Wu Zetian. She was also the 7th daughter of Li Xian, Zhong Zong of the Tang Dynasty. She was sentenced to death by Wu Zetian in the first year of Da Zu (701 A.D.) and was offered Princess Yong Tai in the 2nd year of Shen Long (706 A.D.). Later she and her husband Wu Yanjiwere removed from Luo Yang to Qianling Mausoleum to meet with adjacent. Discovered and excavated in 1960, the tomb is located in Qianxian County, Shaanxi Province. The mausoleum is surrounded by walls. The tomb itself is composed of a passageway, a corridor, an air－shaft, a tunnel and a chamber. It is 87.5 meters in length, 3.9meters in width, and 16.7 meters in depth. On the walls of the passageway and the chamber are painted with worriors, blue dragons, white tigers, palace－like buildings, guards of honour in procession, the display of halberds, plain patterns, clouds and cranes, and waiting men and waiting maids respectively. Especially the two paintings of palace maids painted on the east walls of the front chamber are extremely beautiful and vivid. The painting technique is skilful and the lines are smooth and elegant. They are the masterpieces of the frescoes in the Tang Dynasty.

13. 秉燭宮女 A Palace Maid Carrying a Candle

15

14. 宫女 Palace Maids

17

15. 持高足杯宫女

Palace Maid Holding a High-Stemed Cup

16. 持高足杯宫女(局部)Palace Maid (Part)

17. 領隊宮女 A Leading Maid

18. 宫女 Palace Maids

19. 秉燭宮女 A Palace Maid Carrying a Candle

20. 執拂塵、如意宮女 The Palace Maids Carrying a Duster and an S－Shaped Object

21. 宫女 Palace Maids

22. 捧菓盤宮女 A Palace Maid Carrying a Fruit Tray

23. 二宫女 Two Palace Maids

章懷太子墓 Prince Zhang Huai's Tomb

　　章懷太子名李賢,是高宗李治和武則天的次子,唐文明元年(684年)被武則天流放巴州,後自殺。中宗復位後於神龍二年(706年)以雍王身份陪葬乾陵。景雲二年(711年)追封爲章懷太子,重開墓室,與妃房氏合葬。此墓位於陝西省乾縣,1971年發掘。墓頂封土呈覆斗形,原有圍牆,地下由墓道、4個過洞、3個天井、6個小龕、前後甬道及前後墓室組成,全長71米、寬3.3米、深7米。墓內繪狩獵出行、馬球、儀仗、禮賓、男女侍等壁畫54幅,總計400余平方米。壁畫氣勢宏偉,内容豐富,形象生動,逼真地反映出唐代皇親貴族的生活場景以及當時社會政治、經濟、文化等方面狀況。是研究唐代歷史的珍貴資料,也爲中國繪畫史增添了光輝的篇章。

　　The Crown Prince Li Xian was the 2nd son of Li Zhi, Emperor Gao Zong and Empress Wu Zetian. He was sent to exile in Ba Zhou District in the first year (684 A. D.) of the reign Wen Ming, and later he was compelled to commit suicide. In the 2nd year (706A. D.) of the reign of Shen Long, he was buried in attendant as Yong Wang to Qianling Mausoleum. In the 2nd year (711 A. D.) of the reign of Jing Yuen, he was subsequently endorsed the Crown Prince Zhang Huai. Then the tomb was opened and reburied with his concubine Lady Fang together. Sitting in Qianxian County, Shaanxi Province, the tomb was unearthed in 1971. Above the ground the tomb is covered by the top soil in the shape of a upturned "dou" and was originally surrounded by walls. Under the ground the tomb is composed of a passageway, corridors, 3 air – shafts, 6 small – sized niches, a front and a back chamber. It is 71 meters long, 3. 3 meters wide and 7 meters deep. The chief paintings in the tomb are those entitled on a Hunting Trip, Polo Playing, Guard of Honour in Procession, Foreign Envoys, Waiting Men and Waiting Maids, with the total number of 54 pieces and the total area of more than 400 square meters. All the paintings are magnificent, rich in contents, vivid and true to life. They reflect the sight of the imperial noble life in the Tang Dynasty and the social economic and cultural conditions at that time. The are the valuable material for the study of the history of the Tang Dynasty and they add splendid pieces of paintings to the history of the ancient Chinese fine arts.

24. 狩獵出行(之一)Hunting Procession (part I)

25. 狩獵出行(之二)Hunting Procession（PartⅡ）

26. 狩獵出行（之二局部）Hunting Procession（Part Ⅱ）

27. 狩獵出行(之二局部)Hunting Procession(Part Ⅱ)

28. 狩獵出行(之三)Hunting Procession(PartⅢ)

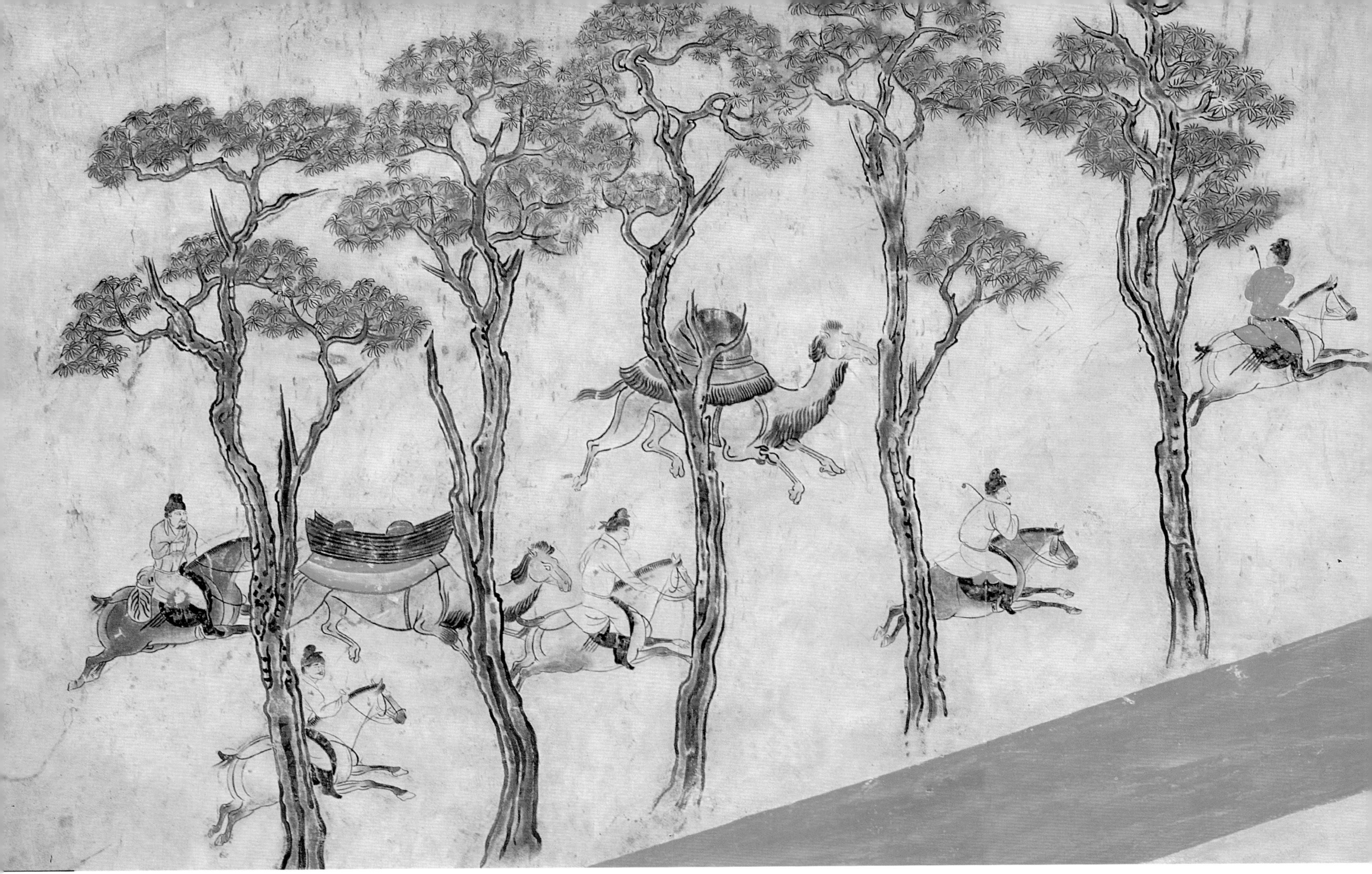

29. 狩獵出行(之四)Hunting Procession(PartⅣ)

30. 狩獵出行(之四局部)Hunting Procession(Part Ⅳ)

31. 馬球(之一)Playing Polo(part Ⅰ)

32. 馬球(之二)Playing Polo(part Ⅱ)

33. 馬球(之三)Playing Polo(partⅢ)

34. 馬球(之四)Playing Polo(Part Ⅳ)

38

35. 樂舞侍女 The Musician and Dancing Maids

36. 執拍板、抱琵琶侍女 The Maidservants Carrying Clappers and Piba

37. 侍女侏儒 The Maidservants and a Dwarf

38. 侍女侏儒(女)A Maidservant and a Male Dwarf

39. 側立侍女 A Maidservant Standing on Her Side

44

40. 觀鳥捕蟬(左)Watching Bird and Catching Cicada(Left)

41. 觀鳥捕蟬(右)Watching Bird
and Catching Cicada(Right)

42. 儀衛領班

Captain of the Guard of Honour

43. 客使 Envoys

44. 禮賓 Receiving Foreign Guests

45. 舞蹈侍女 The Dancing Maid

46.二侍女 Two Maidservants

47. 捧樂器二侍女 Two Maidservants Carrying Musical Instruments

48. 提罐侍女 A Maidservant Carrying a Jug

49. 捧盆景男裝侍女 The
Maidservant in Men's Costun
Carrying a Potted Landscape

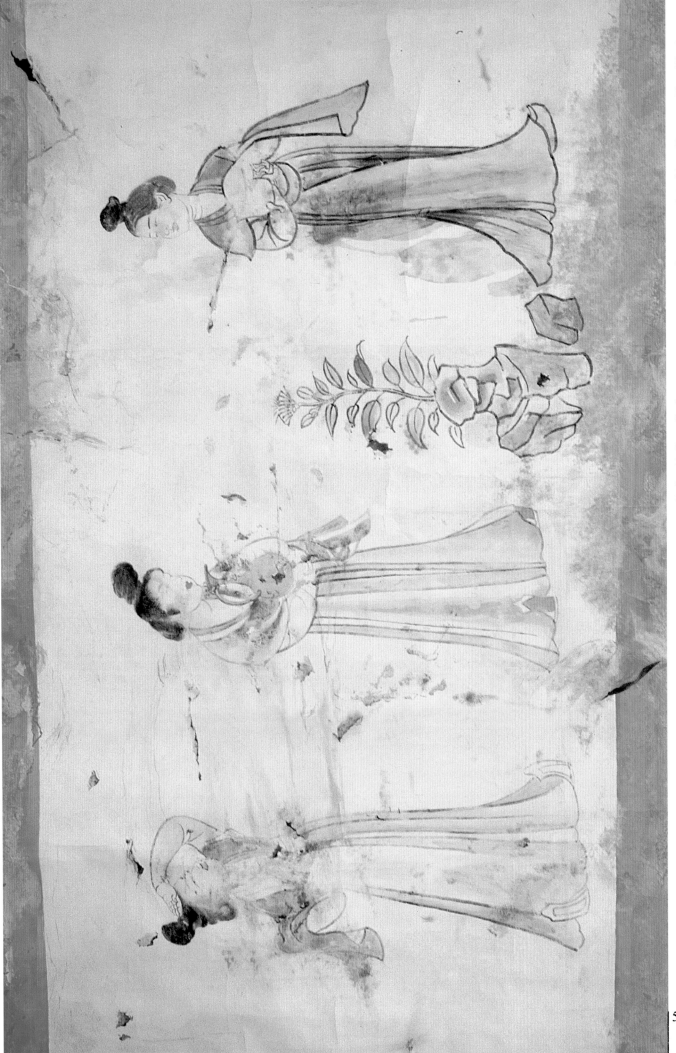

50. 仰觀、捧物三侍女 Three Maidservants Looking up and Holding Objects in Their Hands

55

51. 仰觀侍女 The Maidservant Looking Up

52. 捧壶侍女 The Maidservant Carrying a Pot

53. 捧物侍女 The Maidservant Carrying an Object

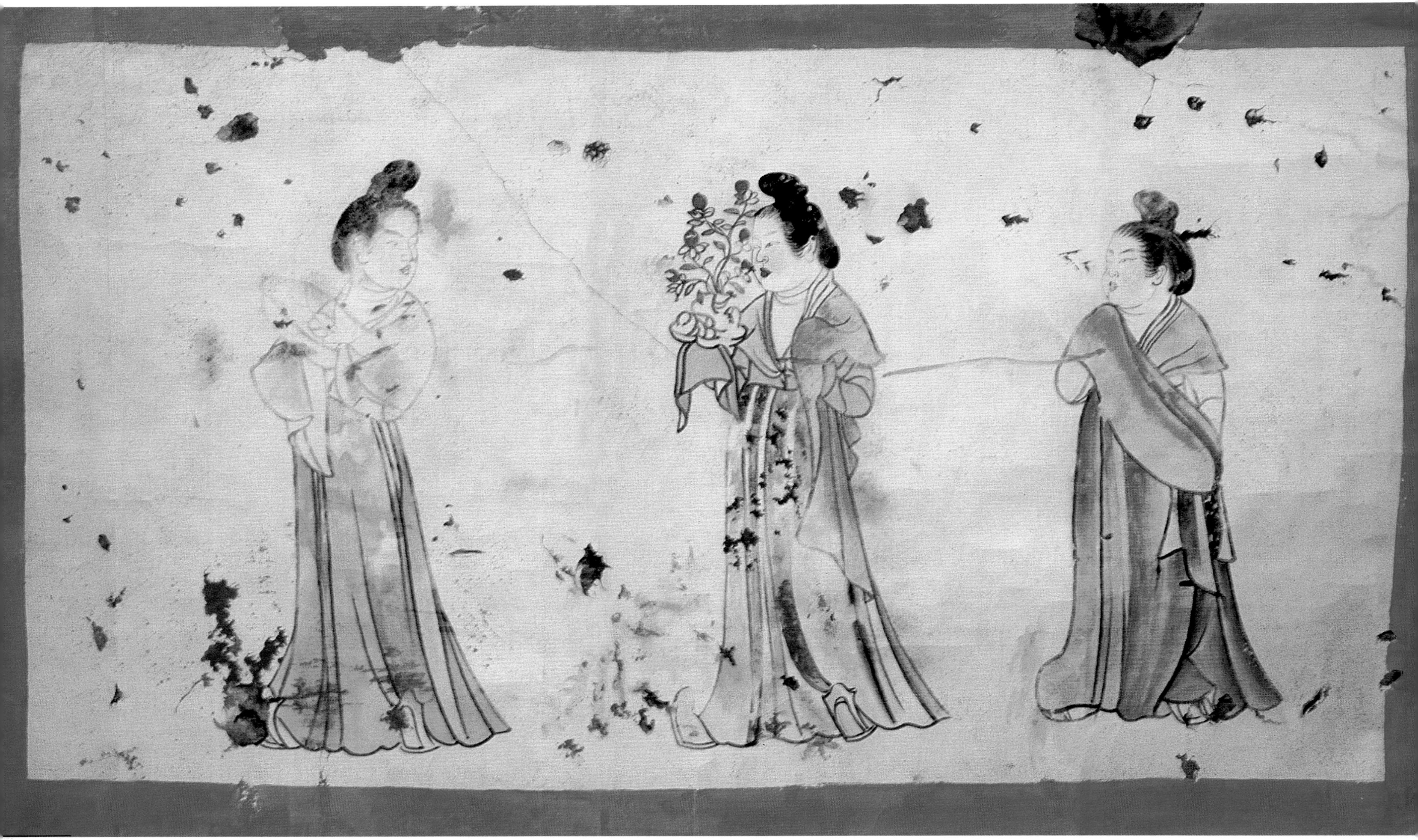

54. 捧花盆三侍女 Three Maidservants Carrying Flower Basins

55. 側顧侍女 The Maid Looking Sideways

56. 侍女給使 A Maidservant and a Waitingman

57. 捧簫侍女 The Maidservant Holding a Xiao(A Bamboo Flute)

58. 領班、整妝侍女 A Foreman and a Maid Decking Herself Out

59. 給使 The Waitingmen

懿德太子墓壁畫 Prince Yi De's Tomb

　　懿德太子名李重潤,是高宗李治和武則天之孫,中宗的長子,唐大足元年(701年)與其妹永泰公主被武則天杖殺。中宗復位後,於神龍二年(706年)將靈柩由洛陽遷至乾陵陪葬,追贈爲懿德太子。此墓位於陝西省乾縣,1971年發掘。墓地有封土和圍牆,地下全長100.8米,由墓道、6個過洞、7個天井、8個小龕、前後甬道和前後墓室組成。墓內繪大型壁畫40幅,有指示方位的青龍、白虎,有表明墓主尊卑等級的戟架和闕樓,有炫耀墓主生前顯赫聲勢的儀仗,有反映豪華享樂生活的伎樂、內侍、宮女等,壁畫內容豐富多彩,構圖嚴謹縝密,色彩鮮艷明快,具有極高的歷史、藝術價值,也是"號墓爲陵"規模較大的一座唐墓。

　　Crown Prince Yi De originally named Li zhongrun, used to be the grandson of Li Zhi, Emperor Gao Zong of the Tang Dynasty, and son of Zhong Zong. In the first year (701 A.D.) the reign of Da Zu, he and his younger sister Princess Yong Tai were beaten to death with a stick at Wu Zetain's order. When Emperor Zhong Zong came to the throne, he was honoured the Crown Prince and his coffin was removed from Luo Yang in attendant to Qianling Mausoleum. The tomb situated in Qian Xian County, Shaanxi Province was excavated in the year of 1971. In the cemetery the tomb is covered with top soil and surrounded with walls. The under ground tomb is 108 meters in length. It is composed of a passageway, 6 corridors, 7 air-shafts, 8 small-sized niches, a front tunnel and a back tunnel meeting with a front chamber and a back chamber. There are 40 pieces of masterpieces of paintings in the tomb. Some are focused on blue dragons, white tigers to indicate the directions. Some are on racks of halberds and palace-like buildings, some are on procession to show the social status and the dignity of the master of the tomb. Some of the paintings are to show the tremendous momentum and the impressive occasions of the Crown Prince, and some are on musicians, eunuchs, palace maids to reflect the luxurious life of the master of the tomb. The mural paintings inside the tomb characterized by the rich subjects, conscientious and subtle figuration, fresh and var;;d colors. They are of great values in history and art. It is also one of the biggest tomb which is named as the mausoleum in the Tang Dynasty.

60. 闕樓 Fortress Towers

61. 儀仗(之一)Guards of Honour (Part Ⅰ)

62. 儀仗(之二)Guards of Honour (Part Ⅱ)

63. 儀仗(之三)Guards of Honour（Part Ⅲ）

64. 馴豹 Leopard Taming

65. 架鵑戲犬 Shouldering a Sparrow Hawk and Playing with a Dog

66. 二宫女 Two Palace Maids

67. 执扇宫女 Maid of Honour with Fan

68. 執扇宮女 Maid of Honour with Fan

韋泂墓 Wei Jiong's Tomb

　　韋泂系中宗韋后之弟,唐如意元年(692 年)卒,景龍二年(708 年)追封爲淮陽王,陪葬榮先陵。該墓位於陝西省長安縣南里王村,1959 年發掘。墓由前後室、甬道、天井、小龕、墓道組成,全長 40.2 米,墓道繪青龍、白虎、朱雀,墓門頂部繪樓閣。甬道及墓室壁畫大都剝落,僅存頂部雲鶴及西壁、北壁的幾幅半身人物畫。

　　Wei Jong, brother of Queen Wei, Emperor Zhong Zong's consort, died in the first year of Ru Yi (692 A. D.) and in the 2nd year of Shen Long (706) was recognized as the king of Huai Yang. After his death he was buried in attendant to Rong Xian Mausoleum. The tomb is located in Nan Liwang Village, Chan'an County, Shaanxi Province. It was discovered and excavated in 1959. The tomb consists of a front and back chamber, a tunnel, an air - shaft, and a small - sized niche. On the walls in the passageway are painted with blue dragons, white tigers and scarlet birds. On the top of the gate way is painted with some tower buildings. Unfortunately, most of the paintings on the walls of the tunnel and the chambers have fallen off except for one piece on cloud and crane on the ceiling and some bust figures on the west and north walls.

69. 抱胡瓶男侍 The Waitingman with a Hun Bottle

70. 高髻仕女 The Waitingmaid with a High Hair Coil

71. 仕女 The Waitingmaid

韋浩墓 Wei Hao's Tomb

　　韋浩，中宗韋后之弟，唐如意元年(692年)薨於容州都督府，神龍二年(706年)追贈武陵郡王，景龍二年(708年)葬於韋曲。此墓位於陝西省長安縣南里王村，1987年發掘。墓內壁畫局部剝落，殘留前墓室東、西壁的高士，甬道及後墓室的侍女、男侍等。墓室頂部、甬道、前室的畫面以及建築物中均滿繪仙鶴和珍禽飛鳥，可見墓主人的生前所好。

　　Wei Hao, brother of Queen Wei, Emperor Zhong Zong's consort, died in the first year (692 A.D.) of Reign Ru Yi in Rong Zhou. He was honoured king of Wu Ling Jun in the 2nd year of Shen Long (706A.D.) and was buried in Wei Qu, Chang'an County in the 2nd year of the reign of Jing Long (708A. D.). With the excavation done in 1987, the tomb was originally located in Nan Ling Wang Village, Chang'an County, Shaanxi Province. Part of the paintings on the walls in the tomb have fallen off except for the intellectual integrity on the west wall and the waiting maids and waiting men on the walls of the tunnel and the back chamber. All the paintings on the top of the tunnel and the front and back chambers and the buildings are focused on cranes and rare birds. All these are enough to reflect the hobbies of the owner of the tomb during his life-time.

72. 鸚鵡侍女 Maidservant with Parrot

73. 喂鳥侍女 The Maidservant
Feeding a Bird

74. 持蒲扇侍女 The Maidservant
Holding a Cattail Leaf Fan

75 高士 High-minded Man

76. 觀蜂侍女 The Maidservant Watching a Bee

77. 花鳥侍女 The Flower, the Bird and the Maidservant

薛氏墓 Madam Xue's Tomb

78. 雙環髻侍女 The Maidservant with Double Ring Hair Coils

薛氏,萬泉縣主太平公主第二女,卒於唐景雲元年(710年)。此墓位於陝西省咸陽市底張灣,1953年發掘。墓由墓道、過洞、天井、甬道、前後墓室組成。墓室壁畫殘損嚴重,過洞、天井、甬道分別繪門闕、戟架、男女侍等。

Madame Xue, the second daughter of Tai Ping Princess of the Governor of Wan Quan County passed away in the first year of JingYun (710 A. D.). It is located in Di Zhang Wan, Xian Yang City, Shaanxi Province. It was excavated in 1953. The tomb is composed of a passageway, a corridor, air - shafts, a tunnel and the front and back chambers. The paintings in the tomb are seriously damaged. On the walls of the passageway the air - shafts, the tunnel are painted with gate buildings, racks of halberds and waiting men and waiting maids.

張去逸墓 Zhang Quyi's Tomb

張去逸,官階銀青光祿大夫,太僕卿上柱國,卒於唐天寶七年(748 年)。此墓位於陝西省咸陽市底張灣,1953 年發掘。墓道原繪的青龍、白虎,甬道及墓室所繪的武士、侍女、男樂隊等均漫漶不清。這幅男樂原壁現已殘損,摹本成唯一的形象資料。

Zhang Qu Yi, took the post of Advisory Official with a Silver Seal and Blue Ribbon, the Highest Meritorious Military Officer. He died in the 7th year (748 A.D.) of the reign of Tian Bao. The tomb is located in Dizhang Wan, Xian Yang, Shaanxi Province and it was excavated in 1953. The paintings on the blue dragons and the white tigers and the paintings of warriors and waiting maids the orchestra are all vague. The original fresco on the male musician has already been damaged and the copy has become the only image material.

79. 男樂 Male Musician

慶山寺遺址 Qingshansi Ruin

　　1985 年 5 月,在陝西省臨潼縣新豐磚瓦廠發現了一座磚砌券室——唐開元二十九年(741 年)慶山寺上方舍利塔下安置釋迦如來舍利的精室,平面呈甲字形,由斜坡道、甬道和主室三部分構成。精室砌築考究,砌磚牆面直接彩繪壁畫,地面又塗朱丹。東、西、北壁分別繪藥師佛與彌陀佛、樂伎、金剛力士壁畫 5 幅。人物綫條流暢,造型準確,姿態各異,是研究盛唐繪畫、樂舞藝術和中外文化交往的寶貴依據。

　　In 1985, in the brick making mill was discovered a brick made vaulted room —— the room to preserve the Sarira of Skt. Tathagata under the Skt. Sarira – stupa in the Qing Shan Temple of the Tang Tynasty. The plane pattern of the room is in the shape of the Chinese character , and it is composed of a slope way, a tunnel and the main chamber three parts. The walls of the room are allexquisitely lain and are painted with colorful paintings directly. The floor is painted with vermilion. On the west walls and the eastwalls are painted with Bhaisajyaguru, the Amitabha , femalemusicians and guardians five paintings respectively. All the lines of the figures are very grace and smooth and the figuration are accurate with different postures. They are the precious records for the study of the painting in the prosperous period of the Tang Dynasty, the music and dance art and the cultural exchanges between China and foreign countries.

80. 高僧 Buddhist Monks

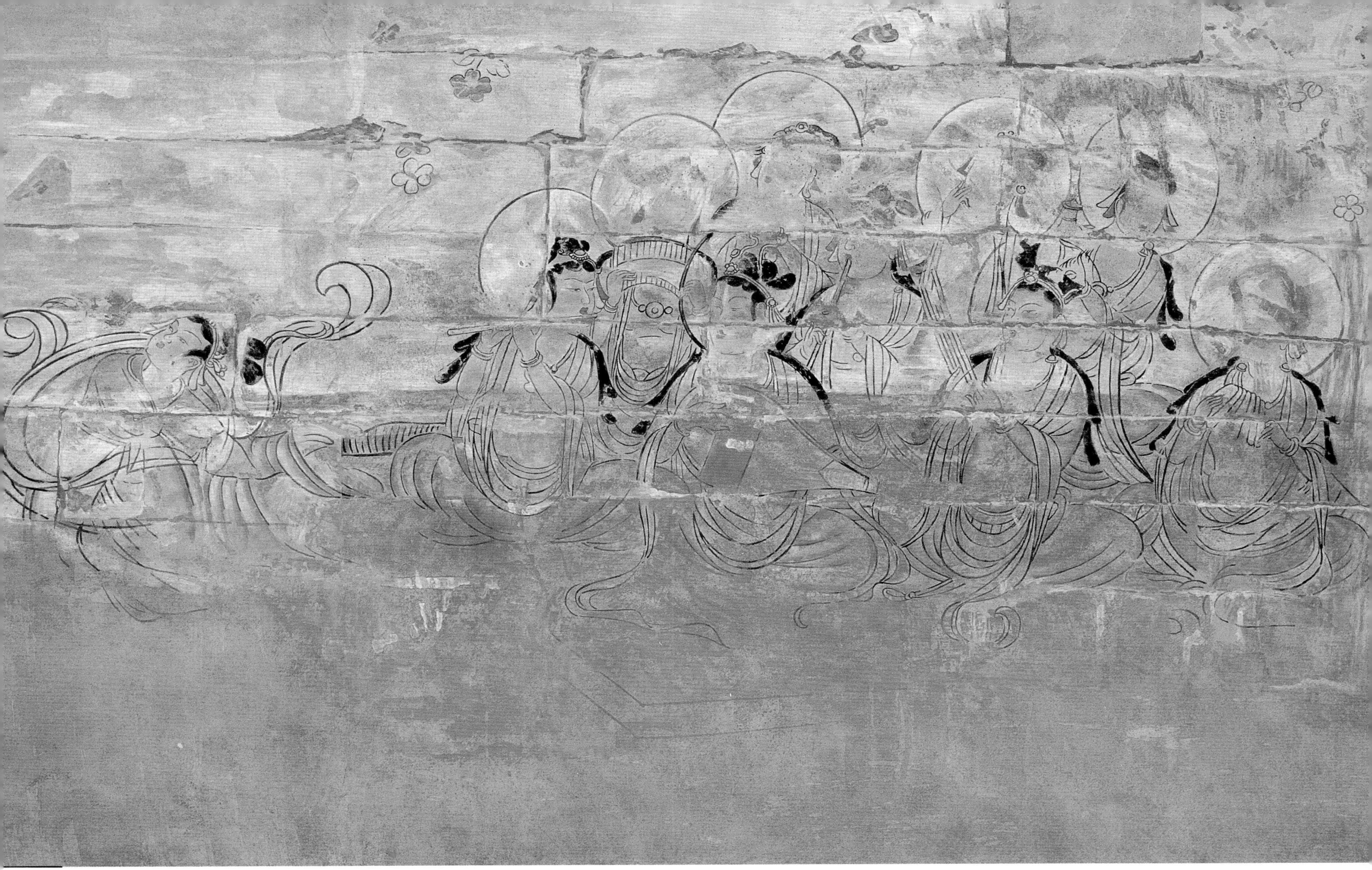

81. 伎樂 Musicians

蘇思勗墓 Su Sixu's Tomb

82. 胡騰舞 Huteng Music and Dance

蘇思勗,官至銀青光祿大夫、行内侍省内侍員外,唐天寶四年(745 年)卒。該墓位於陝西省西安市東郊緯十路,1952 年發掘。墓由墓道、甬道、墓室三部分組成,全長 13.7 米。所繪 24 幅壁畫大都完好。墓室東壁繪樂舞一組,西壁繪六屏式人物畫六幅,南壁繪朱雀,北壁繪玄武及男女侍。畫風近似寫意,筆墨飄灑,敷彩簡淡。特別是東壁的樂舞,舞姿逼真活現,是研究唐代胡騰舞的重要資料。

Su Sixu, held a post of Advisory Official with a Silver Sealand Blue Ribbon, acting as a secondary official of the Bureau of Eunuches. He died in the fourth year of Tian Bao (745 A.D.). The tomb is located in the Wei Shi Road, the East Suburbs of Xi'an City, Shaanxi Province and it was discovered in 1952. It is composed of a passageway, a tunnel and a chamber three parts with a total length of 13.7 meters. All the 23 paintings painted on the walls are preserved in good condition. On the east wall of the chamber is painted a series of paintings of music and dance. On the westwalls are painted with six pieces of vertical scrolls of figures. The south wall is attended with the scarlet bird and while the north wall is painted with the tortoise and snake and some waiting men and waiting maids. The style of the painting exploited by the painter is similar to the freehand brushwork and the lines are graceful and vigorous and the coloration is plain and concise especially the paintings on the east walls entitled Music and Dance are vivid and true to life. They are the significant materials for the study of the Hu Teng dance in the Tang Dynasty.

83. 樂隊(左側) Music Performance (left)

84. 仕女 Palace Maid

南里王村唐墓Nanliwang—cun Tomb

　　此墓位於陝西省長安縣韋曲北原,因未發現墓誌,墓主身份不明。但從這一帶曾是唐代顯赫一時的韋氏家族的墳園,先後發掘過韋洞,韋浩等墓推知,可能是韋氏家族成員。從墓葬規格及隨葬器物看,應屬於中小地主階層。墓室四壁、甬道、穹隆頂上均繪有壁畫。因地勢較高,畫面保存完好,色彩鮮艷。壁畫風格隨意,當出自民間畫工之手。內容寫實,充滿生活氣息。

　　The tomb is located on the north highland of Wei Qu, Changan County, Shaanxi Province. The owner is of unknown identity because the inscription memorial tablet is not found. However, according to the fact this is the cemetery of the illustrious Wei clan in the Tang Dynasty, in which the tomb of Wei Jie and the tomb of Wei Hao are discovered and excavated, we can infer that this tomb belongs to the family member of the Wei clan. According to the scale of the tomb and the funeral objects of the tomb we can see that the owner of the tomb should be from the social status of a middle and small landlord. On the walls of the passageway and the tunnel and the top of the dome are painted with frescoes. Because the position is high, the paintings are preserved in good condition and the colors are fresh. The frescoes are painted at random. They are most probably painted by the folk painters. The contents are realistic and true to life.

85. 朱雀 Scarlet Bird

86. 玄武 The Xuan Wu

唐安公主墓 Princess Tangan's Tomb

　　唐安公主是德宗的長女,皇太子李誦之胞妹,唐興元元年(784年)卒。此墓位於陝西省西安市東郊王家墳,1989年發掘。墓由墓道、甬道、墓室組成。墓室及甬道均彩繪壁畫,除墓室東壁及穹隆頂的天象圖殘脫外,甬道兩壁所繪男、女侍,墓室西壁花鳥,南、北壁的朱雀、玄武基本完好。特別是西壁的花鳥畫,是以獨立的畫面出現,筆墨輕利,天趣猶存,比以往發現的幾幅墓室花鳥壁畫時代均早,可補畫史之缺憾。

　　Princess Tangan was the eldest daughter of De Zong, the Crown Prince Li Song's cousin and died in the first year of Xing Yuan(784 A. D.). The tomb is located in Wang Jia Fen in the east suburbs of Xi'an city, Shaanxi Province and it was unearthed in 1989. It is made up of a passageway, a tunnel and a chamber. On the walls of the passageway and the tunnel are painted with colorful paintings. Except for the paintings on the east walls and the astronomical phenomenon chart on the top of the dome have peeled off, the paintings of waiting maids and waiting men on the walls of the tunnel and the paintings of flowers and birds on the west walls of the chamber and the paintings of scarlet bird and the tortoise and snake are almost in good condition. Especially the paintings on flowers and birds are independent paintings. They are painted skillfully and gracefully and full of wit and humor. They are painted earlier than the paintings on flowers and birds to fill the vacancy of the history of art.

88 . 花鳥 Flowers and Birds

寧夏固原地區 Ningnxia Guyuan Area

89. 溜馬 Walking a Horse

史勿昭墓 Shi Wuzhao's Tomb

90. 武士 Warrior

敦煌 新疆石窟壁畫

THE MURAL PAINTINGS FROM THE GROTTOES IN DUNHUANG AND XINJIANG

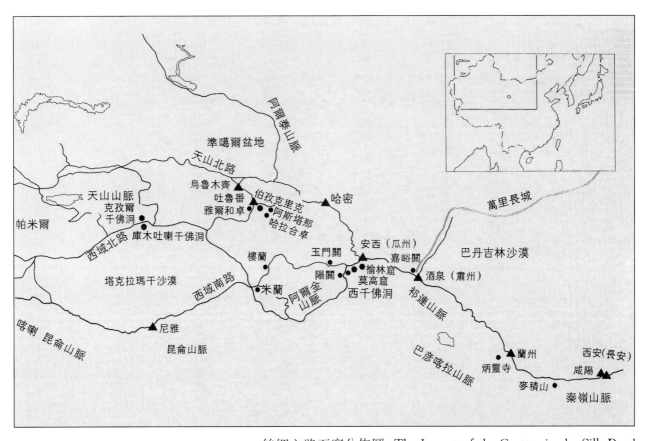

絲綢之路石窟分佈圖　The Layout of the Grottes in the Silk Road

敦煌莫高窟 Dunhuang Mogao Grottoes

　　莫高窟位於甘肅省敦煌縣東南25公里的鳴沙山東麓的崖壁上，上下五層，南北長約1,600米，至今仍保存從公元四世紀至十四世紀一千多年間開鑿的洞窟492個，其中壁畫45,000多平方米，彩塑像2,000余身。是世界上現存規模最大，保存最完整的佛教藝術寶庫。絢麗多彩的壁畫，主要內容是形象化的佛教思想，同時也描繪了當時的一些社會生活實況，表現出大量的各族人民衣冠服飾以及形形色色建築圖樣。在藝術上，既繼承了中國優秀的民族藝術傳統，又吸收和融合了外來藝術精華，博大精深，氣勢宏偉，形成具有敦煌地方特色的中國民族風格的佛教藝術。舉世聞名，是人類稀有的文化寶藏和精神財富。

　　Mo Gao Grottoes are located on the rocks of the east Ming Sha Shan mountain, 25 kilograms to the southeast of Dun Huang County, Gan Shu Province. There are five layers from the top to the bottom. it is 1,600 meters long from the south to the north. Up till now the 492 caves cut in one thousand years ranging from the fourth to the fourteenth century A.D. the 45,000 square meters frescoes and 2,000 color statues have been well preserved. It is the largest, the most completely preserved treasure store of the art of Buddhism. The themes of the colorful paintings are mainly the figurized thoughts of Buddhism and at the same time the social realities at that time. They depict different kinds of dresses and ornaments of different nationalities and the different kinds of designs of buildings as well. Artistically speaking they not only inherit the fine national artistic tradition but also absorb and combine with the fine qualities of the loan art. They are magnificent and deep, tremendous and splendid, to have formed the Buddhism art with the Dun Huang characteristics and with the Chinese national style. It is well known in the world and it is the rare cultural treasure and the spiritual riches of human being.

91. 飛天 An Apsaras

92. 菩薩 Bodhisattva

93. 觀音及供養菩薩 Avalokitesvara and Bodhisattva

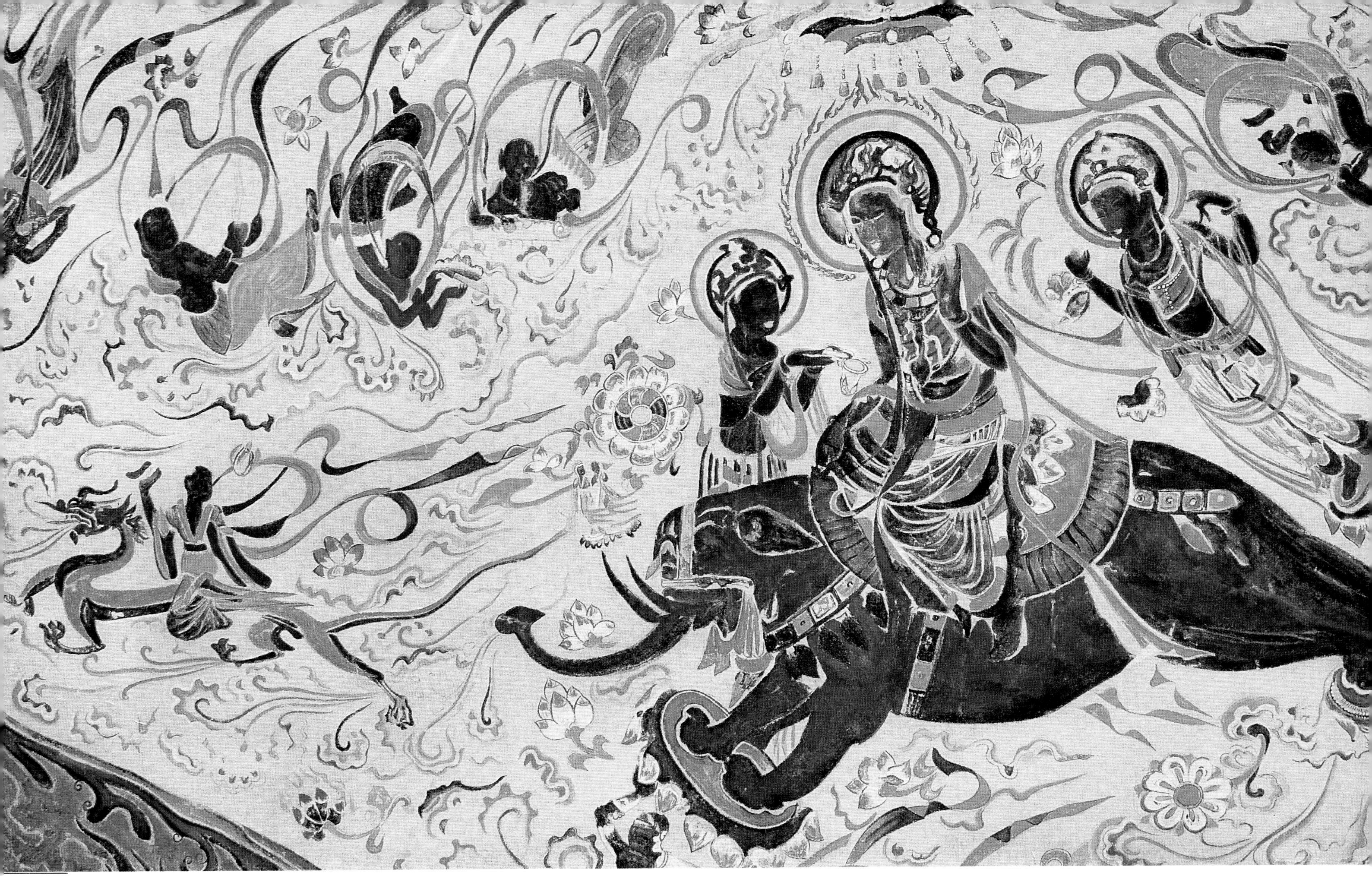

94. 乘象入胎 To Come into Being on the Back of an Elephant

95. 女供養人 A Female Maidservant

96. 化菩薩 Bodhisattva

97. 供養天 Dancing in Pair

99. 女供養人 Female Donor

100. 維摩詰 Vimalakirti

101. 伎樂供養 Deva－musician and Donor

102. 供養菩薩 Servant Bodhisattvas

103. 普賢菩薩 Samantabhadra

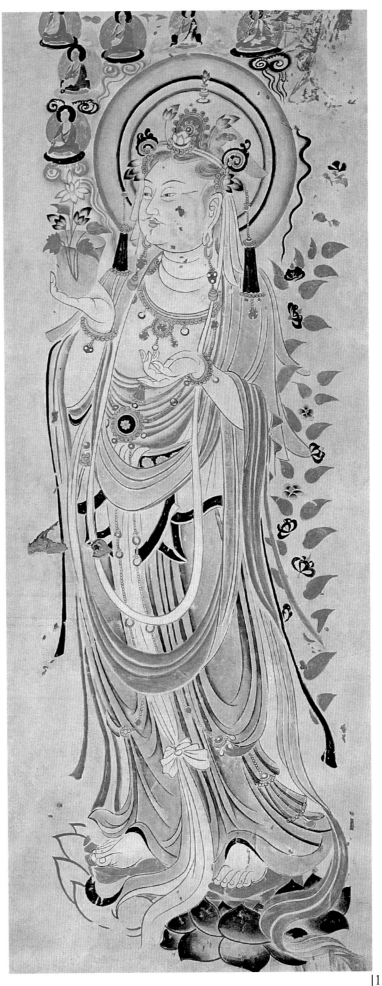

104. 菩薩 Bodhisattva

105. 飛天 An Apsaras

106. 供養菩薩 Servant Bodhisattva

107. 狩獵 Hunting

108. 歡喜金剛 Nandikesvara

109. 南方天王 The Southern Lokapala（敦煌榆林窟 Dunhuang Yulin Grottoes）

110. 供養人 Donors（敦煌榆林窟 Dunhuang Yulin Grottoes）

117

克孜爾石窟 Kezier Grottoes

克孜爾石窟是中國著名的石窟之一。位於新疆拜城東約五十余公里,洞窟鑿於木札提河北岸,明屋達格山的峭壁間。現已編號的洞窟有 236 個,主要是四至八世紀的遺存,大致可分早、中、晚、三期,是龜茲石窟的典型代表。其中洞窟形製較完整,壁畫遺存較多者有 74 個窟,壁畫約有 5,000 平方米。題材主要為佛傳、因緣和本生故事,另外也有反映生產,生活和世俗風情的畫面。壁畫繪製佈局別開生面,以菱形格畫的形式表現,每個畫面,既是一幅表現佛本生故事的完整作品,又起着裝飾壁面券頂的作用。這些精美的壁畫,對研究龜茲社會歷史、佛教藝術及中外文化交流都有着重大意義。

The Ke Zi Er grotto is one of the famous grottoes in China. The grottoes are cut on the steep rocks of Ming Wu Da Ge Mountainon the north bank of Mu Za Ti river about 50 kilometers to the east of Bai Cheng, Xin Jiang Province. Now there are 236 numbered caves mainly the remains of the fourth to the eighth century. They can be divided into three stages, namely the early, the middle and the late stages. They are the typical representatives of the Gui Zi grotto. Among all the caves there are 74 caves are relatively complete and with more paintings with an area of about 5, 000 square meters. The subject matters are mainly the autobiographies of Buddhists, the cause and stories of Jataka, besides, there are also paintings reflecting the production, the life and the custom. The arrangements of the paintings are entirely new. The paintings are arranged in the rhombus checks. Each painting serves as a complete work to express the stories of Buddhism and as a kind decoration to the walls and the tops of the caves. They are of great significance for the study of the social history of Gui Zi the art of Buddhism and the cultural exchanges between China and the foreign countries.

111. 菱形格因緣及本生圖 The Rhombus Check and the Picture of Jataka

112. 本生故事 Jataka Story（Tales of the Buddha's Previous Lives）

113. 菱形格舍身闻偈本生 Rhombus Jataka Paintings and the Jataka Painting

114. 舞伎 Dancing Maid

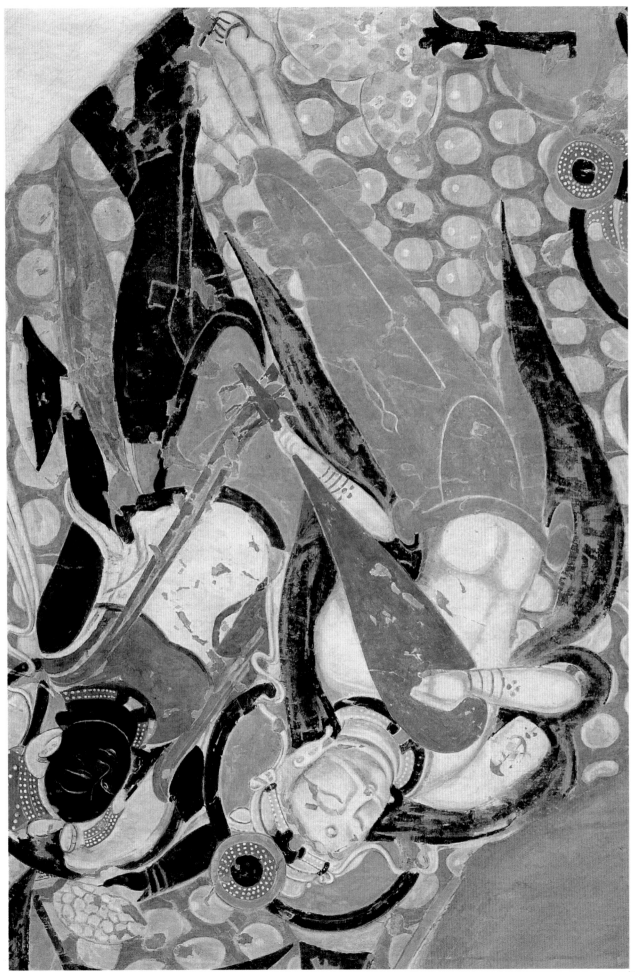

117. 度樂神善愛犍闥婆王 Buddha and Gandharva

118. 度樂神善愛犍闥婆王（局部）Buddha and Gandharva（part）

119. 菩薩 Bodhisattva（庫木吐喇石窟 Kumutula Grottoes）

120. 伎樂 Deva－Musician（伯孜克里克石窟 Turpan Bozikelike Grottoes）

作者簡介 THE BRIEF INTRODUCTION TO THE ARTIST

　　唐昌東,湖北武漢人。1962 年畢業於西安美術學院。畢業後在陝西省博物館工作,早年創作了許多歷史題材的美術作品,後主要從事壁畫的臨摹和研究。從 60 年代起,先後參與并指導永泰公主、章懷太子、懿德太子、李壽、韋浩等大型唐墓壁畫的臨摹及其復原工程。

　　1974 年《中國漢唐壁畫展》首次在日本展出,他組織負責完成唐代部分展品,隨國家文物局局長赴日,參加展覽開幕式,并舉辦了"壁畫摹寫技法"講座。1992 年 5 月,應德國巴伐利亞州文物局邀請,任專家組組長,赴德國爲賽霍夫宮繪製壁衣。同年 10 月,在日本福岡博物館舉辦了《唐代壁畫展》。他所摹寫的壁畫,有些被日本、美國等國的一些博物館、美術館收藏,有些還被作爲貴重禮品贈送國賓。著有《唐代壁畫的創作技巧和藝術成就》(爲《中國壁畫全集·隋唐墓室壁畫》選用)、《唐墓壁畫的臨摹》、《唐代山水花鳥壁畫》、《克孜爾石窟壁畫藝術》、《唐代壁畫的製作工藝》等學術論著。現爲陝西歷史博物館研究員,中國美術家協會、陝西壁畫藝術委員會委員。

　　Tang Changdong born in Wu Han, Hu Bei Province graduated from Xi'an Acadeny of Fine Arts in 1962. After graduation he used to work in the Shaanxi Provincial Museum. In his early years he created many works on the themes of history. Later on he is specialized in the copying and research on the ancient frescoes. From 1960's he has been involved and in charge of the copying of the large-scale frescoes in the tombs of the Tang Dynasty, and has been guiding the restoration work of the frescoes in these tombs.

　　In 1974, "The Exhibition of Chinese Murals from Han to Tang Dynasty" were exhibited in Japan for the first time . He organized and took charge of part of the frescoes in the Tang Dynasty and went to Japan to participate in the opening ceremony with the director of the National Cultural Relics Bureau and delivered lectures on "The Techniques of the Copying of the Ancient Frescoes". In 1992, invited by the director of the Bavaria Bureau, Germany, he went to Germany to paint frescoes for Seeholf Palace as the leader of the expert group. In October in the same year " The Exhibition of Frescoes in the Tang Dynasty" was held in Fukuoka Museum in Japan. Some of his copies of the ancient frescoes have been collected by some museums and art galleries in Japan and the United States. Some of them are presented to the foreign guests as precious gifts. He published The Creating Techniques and the Artistic Achievements of the Frescoes in the Tang Dynasty which is selected by The Complete Collection of Chinese Frescoes in the Tombs of Sui and Tang Dynasties, The Copgying of the Frescoes in the Tombs of the Tang Dynasty, The Frescoes on Mountains, Waters, Flowers and Birds, The Art of the Frescoes in the Kezier Grottoes, The Art of the Creation of the Frescoes in theTang Dynasty and other academic works. He is a research fellow in National Museum of the Shaanxi History and a member of the Chinese Artist Association and Shaanxi Fresco Art Association.

唐昌東近照 The recent photos of Tang Changdong

作者藝術活動 THE ARTISTIC ACTIVITIES OF THE ARTIST

1、1974 年在日本參加《中國漢唐壁畫展》開墓式。

2、在章懷太子墓臨摹壁畫。

3、在絲綢之路考察途中。

4、常書鴻先生同作者親切交談,欣賞壁畫照片。

1. Participating in the opening ceremony of "The Exhibition of Chinese Murals from the Han to Tang Dynasty" held in Japan in 1974.

2. Copying mural paintings in the crown tomb of the crown prince Zhang Huai

3. Investigation on the way of the "Silk Road"

4. Mr Chang Shuhong having an intimate talk with the painter and appreciating photos of frescos

5、1992 年《唐代壁畫展》在日本展出。

6、福岡市長桑原敬一等興致勃勃觀看壁畫展。

7、壁畫展覽盛況。

8、日本著名美術史學家、83 歲高齡的谷口鐵雄先生, 曾三次遠道專程觀看展覽, 與作者合影留念。

5. The Exhibition of Frescos in the Tang Dynasty held in Japan

6. The mayor of Fukuoka and other officials watching the exhibition with great interest

7. The grand view of the exhibition

8. Japanese prominent expert in the art history paid three special visits to the exhibition and took a picture with the painter.

圖版說明

長安、固原墓室壁畫

房陵公主墓 /唐咸亨四年(673 年)

1. 執拂塵侍女 /前室西壁 /高 175、寬 93 厘米

　　頭梳單髻,面龐豐潤,穿白色窄袖衫,紅裙,雲頭履,披巾繞肩,搭左臂肘彎,左肩搭拂塵,雙手輕持拂塵柄端。

2. 提壺持杯侍女 /後室北壁 /高 189、寬 93 厘米

　　梳單髻,體態豐腴,穿白色窄袖衫,紅裙。肩搭綠色披巾,右手提壺頸壺,左手拇指與食指挾持高足杯,作進獻狀。

3. 端菜盤侍女 /前室東壁 /高 175、寬 93 厘米

　　梳單髻,圓臉,紅頰,櫻唇。穿淡黃色窄袖衫,紅裙,雲頭履。深紅色披巾由肩部向後飄垂,雙手端持五足盤至肩側,盤內盛佛手、柿子等菜品。

李壽墓 /唐貞觀五年(631 年)

4. 狩獵 /墓室東壁上欄北側 /高 250、寬 300 厘米

　　本圖係原壁的局部摹本。兩名獵手腰繫箭箙,驅犬架鷹,張弓馳馬在山林追逐射獵。野豬、兔、鹿驚恐逃竄,一中箭的野豬被獵犬擒咬後,仍掙扎狂奔。畫面以簡練的筆墨,刻劃了狩獵時的緊張場景。

5. 騎馬侍衛 /墓道西壁 /高 175、寬 113 厘米

　　此圖為騎馬出行圖中的第二組,第二列,兩騎士均戴幞頭,穿圓領窄袖衫、黑靴,腰繫箭囊,分別騎棗紅和褐色駿馬,勒繮緩行。前者側身回首,顧視後者。

6. 整裝待行 /墓道西壁 /高 196.5、寬 131.5 厘米

　　此圖是出行圖中的一段。圖中七人,拉繮牽馬人絡腮鬍,高鼻深目。馬後六人,或打羅傘,或執雉尾扇,當中的白馬彎頭瞑目,彈動後蹄,束繮垂鐙,鞍韉齊備,靜待主人乘騎。畫面以虛實相生的藝術手法,烘托出墓主人出行威嚴隆盛的氣勢。

7. 樂舞 /墓室北壁 /高 131、寬 160 厘米

　　此圖為原壁貴族庭院內殘存的一組樂舞圖,五名樂伎分別持豎箜篌、箏、琵琶等踞坐毯上專注演奏,後立四人,一執菱網套瓶,一執竹杖。九人均穿白窄袖衫,紅間綠條長裙。舞伎僅見殘存袖、裙一角。

執失奉節墓 /唐顯慶三年(658 年)

8. 巾舞 /墓室北壁 /高 116、寬 70 厘米

　　舞者梳高髻,穿敞胸窄袖衫,繫紅條百褶裙,雙臂揮動紅披巾,身姿宛轉,婆娑起舞。

李震墓 /唐麟德二年(665 年)

9. 戲鴨 /第三過洞東壁 /高 100、寬 84 厘米

　　侍女梳椎髻,穿圓領窄袖衫,下繫白底紅條裙。身姿側傾,低頭俯視,一手提裙,一手揮袖戲逗面前的白鴨。鴨引頸抬頭,張口扇翅,蹣跚挪步。人鴨上下呼應,饒有風趣。

李爽墓 /唐總章元年(668 年)

10. 托盞盤侍女 /墓室西壁 /高 172、寬 89 厘米

　　女侍彎眉秀目,高髻垂環,穿白窄袖衫,繫紫紅裙,雙手托子母盞盤至左肩,臉稍右側,婷婷玉立。

11. 吹笛樂伎 /墓室北壁 /高 196、寬 104 厘米

　　梳雙環髻,穿淡黃色窄袖上衣,外罩紅短袖衫,白底紅條長裙,繫罩綠紗圍腰,足登雲頭履。雙手執一橫笛,正凝神鼓唇,專注吹奏。

12. 舞伎 /墓室東壁 /高 152、寬 233 厘米

　　所摹僅為一對舞伎之一,她頭綰高環望仙髻,穿紅色百戲舞衫,繫黑條紗裙,肩佩彩飄帶,下肢盤旋,上體斜傾,擺動長袖,飛靈起舞。舞姿輕盈飄逸,呈現跌宕起伏的旋律。

永泰公主墓 /唐神龍二年(706 年)

13. 秉燭宮女 /前室東壁北側 /高 179 厘米

　　本圖所繪是宮女圖中的局部,她梳螺髻,袒胸,披綠紗巾,手持蠟燭。在燭光的輝映下,輕紗羅綺透膩指,愈發嫵媚動人。

14. 宮女 /前室東壁南側 /高 176、寬 196.5 厘米

　　畫面九人,為首的梳高髻,手挽披巾,其餘的分執盤、盒、燭臺、團扇、高足杯、拂塵、包裹、如意諸物,隨後徐行。她們彼此顧盼呼應,步履輕盈,儀態萬方。構圖疏密得當,錯落有致。人物形體頎長,綫條灑脫挺勁,色彩濃淡相宜,實屬唐代壁畫藝術之精品。本圖宮女所持團扇、拂塵等物與日本奈良高松冢古墳壁畫里的侍女所持器物類似,反映了當時中日文化的密切交往。

15. 持高足杯宮女

　　這是前圖所繪的一位宮女的特寫。她頭梳螺髻,肩披紗巾,長裙曳地,雙手托高足杯,宛轉身姿,亭亭玉立,風韵卓絶,光彩照人!

16. 持高足杯宮女(局部)

17. 領隊宮女

18. 宮女 /前室西壁南側 /高 179、寬 200 厘米

　　圖中九人,為首一人梳高髻,雙手拱貼腹前,後隨八人分執盤、燭臺、方盒、如意、包裹等物。除最後一人著男裝外,均穿窄袖衫、長裙、披巾、雲頭履。

19. 秉燭宮女

20. 執拂塵、如意宮女

21. 宮女 /前室西壁北側 /高 179、寬 200 厘米

畫面七人，五人長裙披巾，雲笏履，二人男裝。除爲首的宮女外，其餘的從左起依次持燭臺、盞頂函、團扇、菓盤、包袱和鳳首壺。這幅宮女圖原壁已殘損，畫家參照有關形象資料，展現出宮女們各不相同的形態和神韵。

22. 捧菓盤宮女

23. 二宮女 ／前室北壁 ／高 181、寬 134 厘米

前者梳高髻，穿白衫、紅半袖、紅裙、雲頭履，手挽白披巾置腹前；後者梳雙螺髻，穿紅衫、綠裙、披綠巾，雙手捧物，神姿柔美，楚楚動人。

章懷太子墓 ／唐景雲二年（711 年）

24、25、26、27、28、29、30. 狩獵出行（之一、之二、之三、之四） ／墓道東壁 ／分別高 102、149.5、209、174.5、寬 117.5、185.5、160、220 厘米

原圖高 100—200 厘米，全長 890 厘米，揭取時分割爲數塊。整個畫面以松林青山爲背景，四十多個騎馬狩獵者攜弓帶箭，或持馴鷹鞭、或抱犬、或縱鷹、或架鷂、縱馬馳騁。前面有四匹奔馬爲先導，其餘在手持猴旗者後面，前呼後擁，中間一騎高頭白馬的人物，神情嚴肅自若，可能是出行中的主人。殿後的還有兩匹輜重駱駝。構圖氣勢磅礴，場面雄闊壯觀，屬唐墓壁畫中的巨幅傑作。

31、32、33、34. 馬球（之一、之二、之三、之四） ／墓道西壁 ／分別高 196、196、202、225、寬 154、158、104、156 厘米

馬球（也稱波羅球）是古代波斯傳入東土的一種體育運動，唐代在王公貴族階層裏 非常盛行。本圖揭取時分割爲數幅。可見二十多名球手，均戴幞頭，穿窄袖長袍、黑靴、腰間束帶，有的手執偃月形鞠杖。爲首的勒馬躍馬，轉身舉杖擊球。其餘的驅馬競爭，各呈絕技，馳騁穿行在山谷之間。畫面波瀾壯闊，逼真的再現了一千多年前馬毬運動的盛況。

35. 樂舞侍女 ／前室東壁南側 ／高 168、寬 175 厘米

樹左側一男裝侍女，執如意，側身站立；中間宮女背立，高髻，白衫黃裙，紅披巾環肩，手執拍板，扭腰回首顧視；右側侍女高髻，白裙，紅巾，側身領首，懷抱黃布套裝琵琶。

36. 執拍板、抱琵琶侍女

37. 侍女侏儒 ／前室南壁東側 ／高 168、寬 106 厘米

左側侍女體態高胖，高髻，著白衫紫裙；中間爲男裝侍女（眼以上殘），著翻領紅袍；侏儒戴幞頭，著圓領黃袍，疏眉大耳，闊鼻紅唇，爲宮廷豢養的弄人。畫中人物呈階梯狀排列，高低、胖瘦，富於對比。上方一只黃鸝展翅飛翔。

38. 侍女侏儒（女） ／前室南壁西側 ／高 169、寬 106 厘米

畫面繪於影作木構之間。前面的宮女梳高髻，體形肥碩，神情寧靜，穿黃色窄袖衫，綠長裙，披巾，右手貼於胸間，左手繞巾下垂；後邊的宮女梳雙螺髻，粉面朱唇，面帶稚氣，穿綠翻領黃胡服，腰繫帶，窄褲，尖頭履，右手握拳胸前。女侏儒身高僅爲後者的一半，表情痴呆，雙手托黃披巾站在中間。上方有流

雲野雁。

39. 側立侍女

40、41. 觀鳥捕蟬 ／前室西壁南側 ／高 169、寬 175 厘米

原壁畫面爲三名女侍，被摹繪爲兩幅。後面的婦人，左手挽巾，右手執金簪欲插髮髻，忽被空中的飛鳥所驚動，故仰面觀看；中間的少女頭梳雙髻，著男裝，弓腰擺袖，欲捕樹杆上的鳴蟬；前邊的侍女雙手托巾交叉腹前，表情沉靜，若有所思。人鳥樹蟬動靜相錯，藝術構思精巧協和。

42. 儀衛領班 ／墓道東壁 ／高 174、寬 84 厘米

本圖所繪係標準的關西大漢形象。身軀魁偉高大，戴幞頭，穿翻領長袍、戰靴。圓臉短鬚，劍眉星眼，直鼻方口，氣勢軒昂，雙手拄一長劍。綫條挺拔流暢，有"吳帶當風"之式，賦彩單純而富有變化。原壁身後繪有儀衛九人，可知此人係儀衛領班。

43. 客使 ／墓道西壁 ／高 128、寬 65 厘米

圖中人物戴翻沿尖頂帽，闊眉，高顴骨，鷹勾鼻、絡腮鬍鬚、穿紅翻領藍袍、黑靴。一手背後，一手執笏。衣紋綫條清晰，鬚髮用筆精細，暈染厚重，立體感强。可能爲大食國（阿拉伯）使節。章懷太子李賢墓道西壁的禮賓圖原壁已毀，本圖真實的摹繪出原壁客使之一的真容，具有很高的歷史藝術價值。

44. 禮賓 ／墓道東壁 ／高 184.5、寬 242.5 厘米

左邊三人頭戴介幘籠冠，身穿紅色朝服，手執笏板，爲唐鴻臚寺官員。右二羽冠，紅領寬袖白袍，束寬帶，黃靴，爲高麗使節。右三光頭，濃眉深目，高鼻闊嘴，穿翻領紫袍，黑靴，是東羅馬使節。右一可能是中國東北少數民族的來賓。墓主章懷太子李賢，生前曾一度以皇太子的身份主持過軍國政務。本圖不僅印證了這一史實，也是唐與四鄰友好往來的真實寫照。

45. 舞蹈侍女 ／前室西壁北側 ／高 168、寬 175 厘米

樹右側侍女著紅袍，條紋褲，尖頭鞋，左袖高揚，右手背後，傾肩扭腰，翩翩起舞。左側侍女梳高髻，穿白衫綠裙，黃披巾，方頭履，亦步亦趨，右手前伸，呈擊節拍狀。右邊侍女梳高髻，穿窄袖短襦，黃裙，袒胸，手執披巾，雙臂擴展，折腰傾腹，側面站立。

46. 二侍女 ／前室北壁 ／高 169、寬 106 厘米

二侍女相背站立，前者梳高髻，體形肥胖，雙手拱於胸前，側首斜視；後者梳雙髻，身材勻稱，雙手交挽胸前。

47. 捧樂器二侍女 ／前甬道東壁 ／高 106、寬 117.5 厘米

樹石兩側的侍女均梳高髻，穿窄袖衫，長裙，笏頭履。左邊的右手執拍板，側身向後招喚；右邊的雙手捧琴囊，會意的趨步前行。

48. 提罐侍女 ／前甬道東壁 ／高 168、寬 119 厘米

二侍女均穿淡綠窄袖衫，黃裙。後面的雙臂交纏紅披巾於腹前，婷婷玉立，若有所思。前面的肩披綠巾，披巾一端纏左臂，右手提水罐，側身轉首，回眸顧視同伴。畫面以含蓄的手法描繪了侍女的背姿倩影，耐人尋味。

49. 捧盆景男裝侍女 /前甬道東壁 /高 119 厘米

　　侍女眉清目秀，戴襆頭，穿圓領長袍，窄褲，尖頭鞋。雙手翻袖捧盆景站立。女著男裝在唐代頗爲盛行。

50. 仰觀、捧物三侍女 /前甬道西壁 /高 127、寬 198 厘米

　　三侍女均梳高髻，著窄袖衫。左側侍女，面龐圓潤，體態豐盈，袒胸，穿淡黃長裙，右手執披巾一端，左手翻掌舉於額前，凝眸眺望，神態生動；中間侍女，穿綠長裙，披巾，紅雲笏履，雙手捧帶把壺，面對盛開的鷄冠花；右側侍女，穿紫長裙，紅披巾一端從臂間垂下，雙手捧物，似在行進中回首顧視女伴。

51. 仰觀侍女

52. 捧壺侍女

53. 捧物侍女

54. 捧花盆三侍女 /前甬道東壁 /高 127、寬 198 厘米

　　三侍女均梳高髻，穿窄袖衫，黃裙，綠披巾，中間侍女體形豐腴，手捧蓮瓣花盆，下襯黃巾，盆內紅花綠葉，花葉茂盛；右側侍女，面容俊秀，高鼻、櫻唇，雙手捧物至肩側，腰姿宛轉，回眸顧盼；左側侍女，身材矮胖，右手撫巾於胸，左手執巾下端，隨後緩行。

55. 側顧侍女

56. 侍女給使 /後甬道東壁 /高 120 厘米

　　左側給使。旁立侍女體形高大肥胖，高髻，圓臉，紅唇，側身顧視，似爲領班。中間的侍女正在整妝；右側侍女橢圓臉，娥眉鳳眼，直鼻小口，穿白窄袖衫，長裙，黃披巾，雙手捧套裝奩。身旁修竹蔥翠，意境清幽寧靜。

57. 捧奩侍女

58. 領班、整妝侍女

59. 給使 /後甬道東壁 /高 120 厘米

　　給使均戴襆頭，穿圓領長袍，腰束帶，黑靴，前者雙手拱笏；後者拱手相隨。

懿德太子墓 /唐神龍二年(706 年)

60. 闕樓 /墓道西壁 /高 298、寬 302 厘米

　　本圖爲墓主陵園之寫意，主體爲三出闕(一母闕、二子闕)，闕樓均建在梯形的磚砌墩臺上。墩臺棱沿包忍冬蔓草紋石板，并有明顯的收分。樓爲廡殿式，頂有鴟尾，伸檐。面闊及進深各三間，周有迴廊，柱頭斗拱爲五鋪，作雙抄偷心造。座爲單鉤欄的平底斗拱。礅臺與陵園宮牆相接，四周爲山林遠景。

61、62、63. 儀仗(之一、之二、之三) /墓道西壁 /分別約高 326、323、328、寬 224、239、227 厘米

　　此畫表現出太子大朝時的儀仗場面，儀仗隊由車隊、騎馬儀仗隊、步行儀仗隊三部分組成。人馬肅立、車輦排列，旒旗飄動，氣勢雄渾。

64. 馴豹 /第一過洞東壁 /高 192 厘米

　　此圖爲馴豹圖中之一組，馴豹人戴襆頭，穿圓領長袍，腰繫帶，褂小囊，長靴，右肩扛馴豹鞭，左手牽金錢獵豹。獵豹身軀強健，斑毛燦然，神情機警，拖尾闊步與主人同行苑囿之中。唐代獵豹爲西域諸國貢奉，經馴養，專供皇室貴族狩獵用。

65. 架鷂戲犬 /第二過洞西壁 /高 168、寬 133 厘米

　　本圖僅摹繪原壁的右半部分。樹旁站一皇家侍從，戴襆頭，穿圓領長袍，腰繫黑帶，左臂架鷂，右手指劃，側身俯視。頸繫項圈的黃色獵犬，尾巴卷曲，左前爪搭在主人的股上，神態機警敏捷，反映了當時馴養鷹犬的情況。

66. 二宮女 /前室南壁東側 /高 176、寬 115 厘米

　　前一宮女頭梳高髻，著紅色窄袖衫，紫長裙、綠披巾，雲頭履，手挽披巾交叉胸前；後者梳雙環髻，著綠色窄袖衫，長裙，紅披巾，雙手持珠串。圖上起稿綫清晰明顯，設色，綫描淡雅。二者神態矜持、恬美。

67、68. 執扇宮女 /第三過洞西壁 /高 166、寬 129 厘米

　　樹石兩旁各立一宮女，均頭梳高髻，穿窄袖衫，長裙，雲頭履，肩披披巾，雙手持團扇。服色不同，面部表現亦不相同，是皇家宮中掌筵女官的形象，摹繪時將原壁分爲兩幅。

韋洞墓 /唐景龍二年(708 年)

69. 抱胡瓶男侍 /墓室北壁 /高 70、寬 43 厘米

　　男侍戴黑色襆頭，穿紅衫，外罩花領黃袍。闊眉星眼，雙眼皮，高鼻紅唇，下頷微翹，懷抱胡瓶。設色暈染得體，綫條準確雄勁，形神兼備，堪稱一幅成功的男性肖像畫。

70. 高髻仕女 /墓室西壁 /高 94、寬 83 厘米

　　侍女"雲髻巍娥"面頰紅潤，娥眉鳳目，體態雍容，穿紅窄袖衫，披巾繞胸向後飄拂，雙手交於腹前，儀態端莊典雅。

71. 仕女 /墓室北壁 /高 100、寬 92 厘米

　　仕女綰螺髻，圓臉，娥眉秀目，紅頰朱唇，體態豐腴，袒胸，穿淺紅窄袖衫，深紅披巾，手撫披巾，目光斜視。神情矜持恬靜，是唐代婦女的典型形象。

章浩墓 /唐景龍二年(708 年)

72. 鸚鵡侍女 /後甬道北口東壁 /高 80、寬 42 厘米

　　侍女梳雙丫髻，面容清秀，穿唐時流行的胡服，腰繫黑帶，面前有隻鸚鵡，正回首顧盼其主人。

73. 喂鳥侍女 /後室東壁 /高 130、寬 65 厘米

　　侍女戴襆頭，穿翻領長袍，波斯褲，軟便鞋。袍領、袖口和前襟都繡有華麗的花邊。右手提小籠，左手悠然自得的給肩上的金絲鳥喂食，題材活潑有趣。

74. 持蒲扇侍女 /後室東壁 /高 128、寬 65 厘米

　　侍女眉目俊俏，梳螺髻。穿黃色窄袖衫，繫紅裙。披青紗巾，雙手持蒲扇，緩步前行。右上方有隻飛翔的黃鸝鳥。

75. 高士 /前室東壁 /高170、寬260厘米

　　畫面有三位高士漫步於松石叢竹之間，均頭戴竹冠，身穿紅色寬袖大袍。右邊一人拱手獨行；左邊兩人迎面互作手勢，似在清談。三人間以松柏、翠竹、花卉、山石相隔。反映出墓主追慕隱逸生活的精神世界。

76. **觀蜂侍女** ／甬道北口西壁 ／高 76、寬 60 厘米

侍女頭梳螺髻，彎眉秀目，直鼻櫻口，唇注胭脂。雙手拱纏披巾於腹前，靜觀面前一隻低飛的蜜蜂，腦後還有一隻縈迴的蜻蜓。

77. **花鳥侍女** ／後室南壁 ／高 90.5、寬 65 厘米

侍女梳螺髻，穿黃窄袖衫，披綠巾，目光凝視着盛開的鮮花，上方金絲鳥展翅飛翔。好一幅鳥語花香賞春圖。

薛氏墓 ／唐景雲元年(710 年)

78. **雙環髻侍女** ／甬道西壁 ／高 112.5、寬 47.5 厘米

侍女梳雙環髻，瓜子臉，黛眉鳳目，目光側睐，頰施薄粉，唇塗淺脂。穿桔黃衫，青紗裙，手挽披巾，輕貼腹前，折腰顧盼，透出一股嬌憨稚氣。

張去逸墓 ／唐天寶七年(748 年)

79. **男樂** ／墓室東壁 ／高 44、寬 63 厘米

原壁畫面已殘損，應屬多人踞坐奏樂的場面，現僅一人可略窺其全貌。他為胡人形象，八字眉，高鼻，凸顴骨，虬髯。戴幞頭，穿長袍，腰束帶，席地踞坐。雙手按持長笛，聳肩，瞪眼賣勁地吹奏，神情活現，極富感染力。

慶山寺遺址 ／唐開元二十九年(741 年)

80. **高僧** ／精室西壁 ／高 65、寬 94 厘米

圖中五名僧人結跏趺坐於地毯上，觀賞樂舞。前邊一僧，深目，高鼻，為一胡人形象，正凝神觀看。其他幾僧，有的翹手彈指應合節拍，有的靜默聆聽，均沉浸於美妙的樂曲之中。四周繪有花草圖案。

81. **伎樂** ／精室西壁 ／高 69、寬 107.5 厘米

畫面計十名樂伎，均髻束組纓，袒胸露腹，戴項圈腕釧。其中九人分三排結跏趺坐於地毯上，持橫笛、琵琶、笙、拍板、排簫等樂器，專注合奏。前邊一舞伎揮動綢帶，盤旋起舞，舞姿輕柔飄灑。

蘇思勖墓 ／唐天寶四年(745 年)墓

82、83. **胡騰樂舞** ／墓室東壁 ／分別高 142、148、寬 147、137 厘米

原壁揭取時分為三塊。所摹繪的是左側樂隊和中間舞蹈者。樂隊計六人，前排三人分別執琵琶、笙、鈸；後排三人，一指揮，一吹橫笛，一擊拍板。舞蹈者深目，高鼻，虬髯，頭裹巾，穿圓領長衫，腰繫革帶，黑靴。其舞姿據考證係西域傳來的胡騰舞。是研究唐代樂舞的珍貴資料。

84. **仕女** ／墓室北壁 ／高 149、寬 66 厘米

仕女兩鬢抱面，椎髻前傾。臉龐圓潤，兩頰淺施脂粉，眉清目秀，鼻唇匀稱，神情恬靜。穿交衽寬領衫，袖手拱腹，披巾繞肩前垂，體態豐盈健美，典型的盛唐婦女形象。

南里王村唐墓 ／8 世紀

85. **朱雀** ／墓室南壁 ／高 130、寬 99 厘米

朱雀是中國古代南方神祇的象徵，唐墓室裡常繪之以標示方位。圖中朱雀長喙，鷹目，昂首挺胸，展翅翹尾，欲騰空高飛。四周流雲飄動。色彩鮮艷，筆觸開暢，質感很強。

86. **玄武** ／墓室北壁 ／高 170、寬 100 厘米

玄武為龜蛇合體，代表中國古代北方神祇。常繪於墓內標示方位。圖中龜頸長、體圓、足壯，蛇纏繞龜身，尾、頸上交呈一圓環。龜、蛇頭部相對，張口瞪眼相視。四周流雲飛動。

87. **郊野聚飲** ／墓室東壁 ／高 180、寬 235 厘米

中間長方形案上杯盤羅列，案前木墩上置放蓮花形羹盤和曲柄勺。環繞方案有三個木榻，每榻坐三人，均幞頭長袍，正在歡宴暢飲。有的交頭接耳，有的擊掌助興，有的細品咀嚼，有的杯觥交碰，情趣盎然，氣氛活躍。宴席兩旁各有一名端案杯的雙抓髻小童及五名圍觀者，神情各異，生動傳神。背景襯托流雲。畫風粗放自然，近似寫意，人物個性突出，實屬珍貴的歷史風俗畫圖卷。

唐安公主墓 ／唐興元元年(784 年)

88. **花鳥** ／墓室西壁 ／高 180、寬 380 厘米

畫面中間有一木盆，圓口圈足，外髹黑漆，飾貼團花圖案。盆周有四鳥，左起依次為斑鳩、黃鶯、鸚鵡、白鴿，盆上左有二鵲，右有雙雉，均相隨展翅飛翔。兩側各有一株紅梅，樹梢相交畫面頂部。木盆與梅樹之間還有萱草、薔薇、雞冠花卉。畫面清新活潑，富有情趣。花鳥畫在唐以前多作為點綴，裝飾，以花鳥為主體的畫面比較少見。本圖是目前所知有明確紀年的唐代花鳥畫，為中國美術史提供了重要研究資料。

寧夏固原地區

89. **溜馬** ／ ／隋代(581—618 年) ／高 88、寬 114 厘米

牽馬者穿圓領紅袍，黑靴。雙手執馬繮、馬鞭，拱交胸前，側首斜視。馬為淺褐色，驃肥臀圓，剪鬃縛尾，配有鞍韉，正隨主人緩緩行進。

90. **武士**(局部) ／隋大業六年(608 年) ／史勿昭墓天井東壁 ／人物高 166 厘米

武士高鼻深目，翹鬚虬髯，戴高冠，穿寬袖長袍，雙手拄環柄儀刀。神情逼真活現，富有個性特點。隋代墓室畫發現較少，很值得珍視。

敦煌、新疆石窟壁畫

敦煌莫高窟

91. **飛天** ／隋代(581—618 年) ／高 44、寬 65 厘米

兩名飛天遨游雲空，前者揚手散花，後者揮帶騰躍飛舞。周圍祥雲繚繞，情景歡暢。

92. **菩薩** ／隋代(518—618 年) ／404 窟西壁外龕南側 ／高 60、寬 46 厘米

菩薩頭戴花冠，彎眉垂目。左手食拇指拈忍冬花，手勢柔巧，顯得俊逸嫵媚。

93. 觀音及供養菩薩 /初唐(618—704 年) /57 窟南壁中央説法圖東側 /高 100、寬 64 厘米

畫面人物刻畫精細，形象優美。中間觀音頭戴花冠，背有環光，形象豐腴秀麗，細眉長目，直鼻朱脣。冠飾、瓔珞、臂釧均堆金瀝粉，服飾花紋繁麗，五彩繽紛。

94. 乘象入胎 /初唐(618—704 年) /329 窟西壁龕頂 /高 65、寬 102 厘米

乘象入胎是佛傳中悉達多太子(釋迦牟尼)降生的一個情節。白象前後足均踏赤身飛天托持的蓮座，奔馳雲空。菩薩戴寶冠，披天衣，束長裙，安坐象背，兩側有脅侍，前者捧唾盂。乘龍飛天爲前驅，衆飛天環繞相隨。雲騰霞蔚，天花紛飛，氣象萬千。

95. 女供養人 /初唐(618—704 年) /329 窟東壁南側説法圖局部 /高 98、寬 70 厘米

梳"椎髻孤標"髮式，團面豐頰，彎月細目，直鼻櫻脣。穿敞胸圓領窄袖衫，披透明羅巾，束黑裙，手持蓮花，嫻靜地跪在地毯上。綫條凝練，内涵豐富，人物雖僅高 22 厘米，卻被推崇爲敦煌壁畫供養人中的佳作。

96. 化菩薩 /初唐(618—704 年) /334 窟西壁龕内北側維摩詰經變中 /高 69、寬 46 厘米

本圖原繪於維摩詰帳下。化菩薩頭戴寶冠，背有環光，敞胸露臂，赤足，繫長裙，飾飄帶、項圈、腕釧，雙手捧鉢，半跪在蓮花座上，抬頭仰望，神情虔誠。畫面層次豐富，色彩斑斕。

97. 供養天 /初唐(618—704 年) /321 窟西壁龕頂南側 /高 94、寬 66 厘米

本圖以藍天爲背景，上部繪佛一尊，與兩側弟子同坐蓮座，隨祥雲飄浮。雙飛天凌空飛舞，長裙彩帶迎風舒卷。色彩濃艷，層次豐富。下爲六尊散花天人，體態婀娜，憑欄俯視下界。一幅神奇美妙的"天國"景象。

98. 對舞 /初唐(618—704 年) /220 窟南壁阿彌陀經變圖下中部 /高 64、寬 91 厘米

舞者裸上身，赤足，帶花冠項鏈，臂釧、披輕紗，穿黑褲，繫石榴裙，腕釧飾銅鈴，雙手揮彩帶，在小圓毯上呈金雞獨立旋舞狀，舞姿歡快奔放。

99. 女供養人 /盛唐(705—780 年) /敦煌莫高窟 225 窟東壁南側 /高 76、寬 50 厘米

供養人頭纏紅巾，穿紅衫，外罩綠衽白袍，雙手端持長折柄銀鐺，虔誠的跪在地上，綫條洗練，設色素雅。

100. 維摩詰 /盛唐(705—780 年) /103 窟東壁南側維摩詰經變圖局部 /高 94、寬 64 厘米

維摩詰頭扎軟巾，身穿白袍，外罩黑緣紅面披風，赤足坐在胡床上，身微前傾，手揮塵尾，揚眉啓齒，向對方發出咄咄逼人的詰難。綫條剛勁，色彩濃淡有致，刻劃出睿智善辯的居士形象，是莫高窟人物肖像傑作之一。

101. 伎樂供養 /中唐(781—847 年) /159 窟西壁北側文殊變下部 /高 88、寬 66 厘米

三名伎樂天人正聚精會神地演奏。中間的手擊拍板；左邊的吹橫笛；右邊的吹笙。

102. 供養菩薩 /中唐(781—847 年) /159 窟文殊變中局部 /高 43、寬 36 厘米

三名供養菩薩戴花冠、耳環、項圈、臂釧、腕鐲，繫裙褲，披絲帛，裸上身，赤雙足，捧持羹碗、淨瓶，半跪在蓮墊上。均眉清目秀，儀態端莊，軀體似玉，充滿青春活力。

103. 普賢菩薩 /中唐(781—847 年) /159 窟普賢變 /高 100、寬 63 厘米

普賢團面長耳，曲眉垂目，紅脣，有髭鬚，衣飾華麗，氣度雍容。左手托盤花，結跏趺坐在象座上，畫面色彩淡雅，綫條精細，藝術水準很高。

104. 菩薩 /中唐(781—847 年) /199 窟西壁龕北側 /高 124.5、寬 50 厘米

形體高大，面形豐圓、眉目疏朗，小髭鬚，腦後有光環。敞胸，戴寶冠、耳墜、項圈、腕鐲，披帛，束羊腸裙。右手托插花杯，赤足立於三品蓮座上。衣折細膩，神彩飄逸，綫條挺勁，設色柔和，反映出莫高窟中唐時期的一種新畫風。

105. 飛天 /中唐(781—847 年) /158 窟西壁涅槃 /經變局部 /高 84, 寬 61.5 厘米

飛天高髻，勒抹額，團面大耳，細眉垂目。繫綠裙、褐褲、披彩帛，上身赤裸，戴耳墜、項圈、臂釧、腕鐲。手持瓔珞，昂首挺胸，折腰轉身，姿態柔美，飄浮雲空。右上有一雁銜菡萏。

106. 供養菩薩 /晚唐(848—906 年) /220 窟北壁樂師經變局部 /高 58、寬 37.5 厘米

她戴嵌珠抹額及釧、鐲、乳飾，穿棱格褲，披絲帛，裸上身，恬靜地跪坐在池旁的蓮座上。左手拈花蕾，抬頭凝視樂師法身的化像。池中鴛鴦戲水，充滿清新的生活氣息。

107. 狩獵 /晚唐(848—906 年) /156 窟東壁南側下層張議潮出行圖局部 /高 44.5、寬 59.5 厘米

原野遼闊，遠山影映，小鹿、狐狸驚慌奔逃，兩名獵手張弓搭箭，馳馬急追，一副緊張的狩獵場面躍然壁上。

108. 歡喜金剛 /元代(13—14 世紀) /465 窟 /高 64、寬 48.5 厘米

此畫以密宗爲題材，是釋迦牟尼爲調伏欲界衆生而顯示的雙身像之一。主尊藍灰色，戴銀胄，束圍裙，項飾髑髏串，三目六臂，其中雙臂懷抱佛母。佛母肉色，高髻披髮，勒抹額，赤身裸體，雙臂摟主尊頸項，左腿跨主尊右腿上。畫面色調柔和，藝術效果含蓄。

敦煌榆林窟

109. 南方天王 /唐代(7—9 世紀) /15 窟東壁南側 /高 91、寬 68 厘米

天王穿彩繪甲胄，戰靴，繫披風，披彩帶，腰扎獸面扣帶，腦

137

後有環火背光。握箭挎弓,坐在兩上肌肉堅實的惡鬼肩上,神情威武儒雅。身後有打扇小鬼,左上方有小飛天。

110. 供養人 /五代(10世紀) /高117、寬79厘米

前排爲四貴婦,滿頭花飾金釵,兩鬢抱面,濃妝艷抹,貼花鈿,畫花子。遍身羅綺,珠光寶氣,虔誠的拱袖站立。據長框題款知爲某大家之故新婦,新婦及其兩侄女之形象。後四侍女分列兩排,其中二人挾持團扇。

新疆拜城克孜爾石窟

111. 菱形格因緣及本生圖 /晉—南北朝(3—6世紀)38窟主室券頂束側壁局部 /高44、寬62厘米

菱形格畫是龜茲壁畫藝術的突出特點之一。克孜爾石窟壁畫洞窟幾乎都繪有菱形格的畫。本圖左爲快目王施眼本生,右爲屍毗婆梨仙人修忍辱本生。

112. 本生故事 /(局部)晉—南北朝(3—6世紀) /17窟 /高63、寬43厘米

在菱格畫面中繪制出獼猴以身作橋的主題。以綠草坪點綴團花爲襯地。下部繪小河,河兩岸各有一樹,一白毛猴前後雙爪緊緊握持河岸兩樹的樹杆,身軀平伸成橋。一藍一黑二猴踏其身軀渡河,另一白毛猴立河北岸樹上呈接應狀。菱格上部還有一棵樹。

113. 菱形格舍身聞偈本生 /晉—南北朝(3—6世紀) /38窟主室券頂西側壁局部 /高44.5、寬61厘米

左側菱形格内是一切施王本生。一切施王將已身舍於婆羅門,并自縛隨行。右側菱格内是舍身聞偈本生,一半裸者從樹上跳下,右側立一夜叉。

114. 舞伎 /南北朝(5—6世紀) /8窟 /高98、寬65厘米

菱形格畫面里,繪一赤身裸體的舞女,向佛挑逗。舞女體形豐盈,含胸扭胯,嬌柔作態,活現了人生的情態。是古代人體藝術的典範之作。

115. 本生故事 /唐代(7—9世紀) /118窟 /高45、寬78厘米

在菱形格構圖中,一伎樂菩薩正彈奏阮咸。隨着清柔婉妙的旋律,四周之鳥歡飛和鳴,一派升平祥和氣象。

116. 伎樂 /南北朝(5—6世紀) /第8窟主室項部 /高109、寬82厘米

菱格畫面以紫色嵌白卵石爲襯底,繪兩尊伎樂菩薩,前膚色白,後黑,背均有環光,戴手釧,佩飄帛。前者戴珠冠,穿綠褲,雙手抱琵琶,扭腰轉胯,身姿旋爲弧形,雙腳交叉。後者雙手各托一花盤。色彩濃淡暈染,綫條鐵勾銀勒,十分和諧統一,使人物有"身若出壁"的立體感。

117. 度樂神善愛犍闥婆王 /晉—南北朝(3—6世紀) /13窟 /高153、寬93厘米

描繪佛度樂神善愛的故事。善愛犍闥婆王爲八衆之樂神,恣肆,不敬佛法。佛乃化身與之比賽演奏箜篌,善愛自愧不如,遂虔心皈依佛教。畫中右立持箜篌的是善愛。左邊白膚色全裸的則是佛化成的樂神,交腳站立,一臂搭在善愛肩上,神情溫柔安謐,充滿了世間人情味。

118. 度樂神善愛犍闥婆王(局部)

新疆庫車庫木吐喇石窟

119. 菩薩 /北朝(4—6世紀) /21窟 /高88.5、寬62厘米

此窟穹頂共有十三幅菩薩像,呈放射狀排列,這是其中的一幅。菩薩團面大耳,彎眉細目,直鼻厚唇,上唇留蝌蚪形髭,頭髮卷曲,披垂雙肩。頭戴寶冠。飾項鏈,瓔珞,臂釧,繫土紅色花裙。雙手展嵌珠玉帶,身姿優美挺秀。形象豐滿,綫條挺勁,色彩鮮艷,充分體現了古代龜茲的民族藝術風格。

新疆吐魯番伯孜克里克石窟

120. 伎樂 /元代(13—14世紀) /54窟,高76、寬52厘米

這名奏樂者,頭戴花冠,披帛繫裙,裸上身,赤足。頸、臂、腕、踝均戴釧飾。面形豐滿,直鼻朱唇,彎眉合目,結跏趺坐在圓毯上,持鳳首箜篌演奏。

INTRODUCTION TO THE PHOTOGRAPHS

Frescoes from the Tombs in Changan and Guyuan

Princess Fangling's Tomb   Tang(673AD)

1. Maidservant Holding a Duster   On the West Wall of the Front Chamber   Height: 175cm, Width: 93cm

The plump and smooth – skinned maidservant with her hair done in a single coil wears a white color tight – sleeved shirt, a red skirt, a pair of cloud – shaped shoes and a shawl. With one end of the shawl coming down to her left elbow and the duster against her left shoulder, she holds the handle of the duster lightly before her chest.

2. Maidservant with Cup and Pitcher   On the North Wall of the Back Chamber   Height: 189cm , Width: 93cm

The plump – figured maid with her hair done in a single coil is dressed in a white tight – sleeved shirt and a red skirt. With a blue shawl over her shoulders, she carries a long – necked flag on with a crest – shaped spout with her right hand and a high – stemmed cup with her index and middle fingers. She looks to be ready to serve the dinner.

3. Maidservant Carrying a Fruit Tray   On the North Wall of the Chamber   Height: 175cm, Width: 93cm

She has a single hair coil on her head, a round face, rosy cheeks and rouged lips. She is dressed in a light yellow tight – sleeved blouse, a red skirt and a pair of cloud – shaped shoes. With the dark red shawl waving backward, she carries a five – legged fruit tray to the front of her shoulders. On the tray are several fingered citrus and persimmons etc. She looks ready to present the fruits to her master.

Li Shou's Tomb   Tang(631AD)

4. Hunting   On the North Side of the Above Rallings of the East Wall of the Chamber   Height: 250cm, Width: 300cm

This is the partial copy of the original fresco. Two hunters with quivers hanging down from their waists, dogs running ahead, hawks standing on their shoulders, gallop on horse back stretching their bows to chase animals in front. The wild boars, the rabbits and deer are so frightened that they tried to run away in all directions. Though the wild boar shot by an arrow is bitten by the dog, it is struggling to escape desperately. Though the fresco is simple, yet it best demonstrates the tense scene of hunting.

5. The Imperial Guards on Horse Back   On the West Wall of the Passage Way   Height: 175cm, Width: 113cm

This fresco is the second row of the series of the riding procession. Both the riders wear turban – hats, round – collared tight – sleeved robes, black boots, waistbands. They have quivers hanging down from their waists. They are riding a claret horse and a brown one respectively and they are holding the reins tight to walk slowly. The front rider turns back to look at his back companion.

6. Ready and Wait to Start Out   On the West Wall of the Passageway   Height: 196.5cm, Width: 131.5cm

This copy is only one part of the original fresco of ready and wait to start out. There are seven people in the fresco. The man who is leading the horse has thick whiskers, a prominent nose and sunken eyes. Among the six servants following the horse, some are holding umbrellas, some are holding pheasant – feather fans. The white horse in the middle bends down his head and opens his eyes wide and kicks backward with one of his rear hoofs. With the reins of the horse tied and the stirrups hanging down, the saddle and the saddle cloth ready, he is waiting his master quietly to set out on a journey. The true and false painting method is employed to set off the majestic, splendid atmosphere of the master of the tomb.

7. Music and Dance   On the North Wall of the Chamber   Height: 131cm, Width: 160cm

This fresco is one part of the original music and dance fresco in the courtyard of the noble. Five female musicians hold vertical diabolo, zheng, piba etc respectively in their hands sitting on their knees on the carpet playing musical instruments attentively. Four people stand behind them. Among them, one holds a rhombus meshbottle, and one holds a bamboo stick. All the nine wear white tight – sleeved shirts, red and green long stripped skirts. Only a corner of the remaining sleeve and skirt of the dancing maid can be seen.

Zhishi Fengjie's Tomb   Tang(658AD)

8. Shawl Dance   On the North Wall of the Chamber   Height: 116cm, Width: 70cm

The dancer, with her hair dressed in a single coil, is dressed in a decollete, tight – sleeved shirt, and a red stripped long skirt. She waves the shawl with both her two arms dancing smoothly and gracefully.

Li Zhen's Tomb   Tang(665AD)

9. Playing with a Duck   On the East Wall of the Third Corridor   Height: 100cm, Width: 84cm

The maid, with her hair done in a vertebra – shaped coil, wears a round – collared tight – sleeved shirt and a red stripped skirt with white background. She tilts her body to one side and lowers her head to look at the duck with one hand pulling up her skirt and the other waving her long sleeve to play with the duck in front of her. The duck cranes its neck, raises its head, opens its mouth and flaps its wings walk haltingly. It is full of wits and humor and very interesting.

Li Shuang's Tomb   Tang(668AD)

10. A Maidservant Carrying a Tray   On the West Wall of the Chamber   Height: 172cm, Width: 89cm

The maidservant has crescent eyebrows and beautiful eyes, a high hair coil and two ear rings. She wears a white tight – sleeved shirt a purple skirt. She carries a tray on which there are some cups with her two hands to her left shoulder and tilts her face to the right a little bit standing there gracefully.

11. Maidservant Playing the Flute   On the North Wall of the Chamber   Height: 196cm, Width: 104cm

With her hair done in double – ring coils, she wears a cream – colored tight – sleeved shirt covered with a red short – sleeved blouse, a long stripped skirt, a green – gauze waistband and a pair of cloud – shaped shoes. She holds a horizontal bamboo flute with her two hands with her two lips pouting blowing attentively.

Li Ji's Tomb   Tang(669AD)

12. A Dancing Maid   On the North Wall of the Chamber   Height: 152cm, Width: 233cm

The copy is only one of the pair of the dancing girls. She has her hair done in a shape of high ring fairy – watching coil. She wears a red dancing shirt, a black stripped skirt, and a color band over her shoulders. With her lower limbs whirling and upper limbs tilting to one side, she waves her long sleeves dancing lightly and gracefully. Her dancing is lithe and elegant, presenting the flowing rhythms.

Princess Yongtai's Tomb   Tang(706AD)

13. A Palace Maid Carrying a Candle   On the North Side of the East Wall of the Front Chamber   Height: 179cm

The copy is one part of another fresco of palace maids. She wears a snail – like coil on her head, with her chest uncovered, a green gauze shawl carries a candle in her hand. In the candle light, her smooth skin can be seen through the transparent gauze. This adds beauty to her loveliness and attraction.

14. Palace Maids   On the South Side of the East Wall of the front Chamber   Height: 176cm, Width: 196.5cm

There are nine maids in the fresco. The one in the front wears a high coil on her head and draws her shawl with her hands. The other carry a tray, a box, a candlestick, a round fan, a cup, a duster, a parcel, a ru yi(an S – shaped object) etc. respectively in their hands walking slowly forward. They are looking at each other, walking lightly and elegantly with different postures. The composition of the picture is arranged appropriately. The figures are slender of stature. The density of the color is appropriate. The lines are free and easy. It is really the masterpiece of art in Tang Dynasty. The round fans held by the palace maid in their hands is similar to those depicted in the frescoes of GaoShong tomb Nai Liang Japan, reflecting the close Sino – Japan cultural exchanges at that time.

15. Palace Maid Holding a High – Stemed Cup

This is the feature of the previous fresco of palace maids. She, with her hair done in a snail – shaped coil, with a shawl over her shoulders, a long skirt hanging down to the ground, twists her body, holds a high – stemed cup in her hands to present the soft, smooth curved lines of her body. She is very charming and brilliant.

16. Palace Maid (Part)

17. A Leading Maid

18. Palace Maids   On the South Side of the West Wall of the Front Chamber   Height: 179cm, Width: 200cm

There are nine maids in the fresco. The front one wears a high coil on her head with her two hands cupped and placed before her abdomen. The eight maids following her carry a tray, a candle stick, a square box, a ruyi (an S – shaped object), a parcel etc. respectively. They all are dressed in tight – sleeved shirts, long skirts, shawls and cloud – shaped shoes except the last one in men's costume.

19. A Palace Maid Carrying a Candle

20. The Palace Maids Carrying a Duster and an S – Shaped Object

21. Palace Maids   On the North Side of the West Wall of the Front Chamber   Height: 179cm, Width: 200cm

There are nine maids in the fresco. Among them five are dressed in long skirts, shawls and cloud tablet – shaped shoes; two are dressed in men's costumes. Except the first one the others from the left to the right, carry a candle stick, a round fan, a fruit tray, a parcel and a phoenix head pot respectively. The original fresco is damaged. The painter, with reference to some materials of the figures of the palace maids displays the different postures and romantic charm of the maids.

22. A Palace Maid Carrying a Fruit Tray

23. Two Palace Maids   On the North Wall of the Front Chamber   Height: 181cm, Width: 134 cm

The front one has a high hair coil on her head. She wears a red short – sleeved shirt, a red skirt and a pair of cloud – shaped shoes. She places her hands wrapped with the shawl before her abdomen. The one at the back has her hair done in a shape of double snail coils. She wears a red shirt, a green skirt, a green shawl over her shoulders, carrying an object with her two hands. Her figure is smooth and charming.

Prince Zhanghuai's Tomb   Tang(711AD)

24.25.26.27.28.29.30 Hunting Procession (Part Ⅰ Part Ⅱ Part Ⅲ Part Ⅳ)   On the east Wall of the Chamber   Height: 102, 149.5, 209, 174.5cm, Width: 117.5, 185.5, 160, 220cm Respectively

The original fresco was 100cm – 200cm in height and 890cm in length. It was cut into several pieces when taken down from the wall. Against the background of green hills and pine forest, are the more than forty mounted hunters some of whom are carrying bows and arrows, some are holding training panther whips, some are driving hawks and some are carrying sparrow hawks on their shoulders, galloping. There are four leading horses. The others behind are holding monkey flags. With so many attendants crowding around sits a man with solemn and calm expression on a white horse back. Probably he is the master of the tour. Two camels loaded with impediment brings up the rear. The fresco is full of tremendous momentum and the sight is magnificent. It is the masterpiece of art in the Tang Dynasty.

30.31.32.33.34 Playing Polo (Part Ⅰ Part Ⅱ Part Ⅲ Part Ⅳ)   On the West Wall of the Passageway   Height: 196, 196, 202, 225cm, Width: 154, 158, 104, 156cm

Respectively Polo, a kind of sport, came to the Orient from ancient Persia. In theTang Dynasty it was very popular among the nobles. When it was taken down from the walls it was divided into several pieces. Over twenty players, with turban – hats on their heads, wearing tight – sleeved robes, black boots, waistbands, carrying moon – shaped sticks can be seen. The first one reins the horse tight and turns his body to strike the ball. The others are galloping to compete voilently, presenting their excellent skills. They are galloping along the mountain valley. The picture is of a magnificent sweep, reflecting truely the grand sight of the horse polo one thousand years ago.

35. The Musician and Dancing Maids   On the South Side of the East Wall in the Front Chamber   Height: 168cm, Width: 175cm

On the left side of the small tree is a maid in men's costume, carrying a ru yi(an S – shaped object) in her hands, standing on his side. The maid in the middle standing with her back facing the

his side. The maid in the middle standing with her back facing the audience, wearing a high hair coil, a white shirt and a yellow skirt, with a red shawl around her shoulders, carries a clapper in her hand and twists her back to look back. The maid on the right wears a high hair coil on her head, a white skirt, a red shawl standing there on her side and with her head lowered, carries a piba in a cloth bag in her two arms.

36. The Maidservants Carrying Clappers and Piba

37. The Maidservants and a Dwarf　　On the East Side of the South Wall in The Front Chamber　　Height: 169cm, Width: 106cm

On the left stands a tall and plump woman, wearing a high hair coil on her head, a white blouse and a purple skirt. The maid in the middle in men's dress (the parts above her eyes are damaged), wears a red robe with a collar upturned. The dwarf wears a turban — hat, a round collar yellow robe. He has sparse eyebrows and big ears, a wide nose and red lips. He is obviously a clown groomed in the court for entertainment. The three figures in the fresco are arranged according to their height and weight. Their different heights forms an oblique line. An oriole is flying over their heads.

38. A Maidservant and a Male Dwarf　　On the South Side of the West Wall in the Front Chamber　　Height: 169cm, Width: 106cm

The fresco is painted between columns of dou gong. The maid in the front with a high hair coil is very plump. She wears a yellow tight — sleeved shirt, a long green skirt, a shawl with her right hand placed against her breasts, and her left hand hanging down with the shawl around and looks very quiet. The maid at the back, with double snail — shaped coils, a white powered face, rouged lips, expresses childishness on her face. She wears a Hun robe with the collar upturned, a waistband, tight trousers, and a pair of sharp — headed shoes holding her right hand against her chest. The female dwarf is half as tall as the maid at the back. Her expression is dull. She carries a yellow shawl with her two hands standing in the middle. There are flowing clouds and wild geese flying over their heads.

39. A Maidservant Standing on Her Side

40.41 Watching Bird and Catching Cicada　　On the South Side of the West Wall of the Front Chamber　　Height: 169cm. Width: 176cm

The original fresco depicts three maidservants. When it is copied it is painted into two copies. The maid behind holds her shawl with her left hand and carries a gold hair pin in her right hand and she is ready to put it in her hair coil. Suddenly she is frightened by a flying bird in the sky, so she looks up at the bird. The young girl in the middle, in men's dress, with her hair done in the shape of double coils, bends down and waves her sleeves to catch the chirping cicada on the branch trunk of a tree. The maid in the front, with her hands wrapped with the shawl intersected and placed against her abdomen is quiet as if she was in deep thought. The static and the dynamic states of the people, the birds the tree and the cicada are strewn in well arranged order and the composition of the picture is delicate and harmonious.

42. Captain of the Guard of Honour　　On the East Wall of the Passageway　　Height: 195cm, Width: 69.5cm

The figure painted in the fresco is typical of a giant from Western Shaanxi. He is of strong and tall built, wearing a black turban — hat, a long robe with upturned collar and a pair of battle boots. With a round face short whiskers, dashing eyebrows and tiny eyes, a straight nose and a square mouth he rests his hands on the handle of a long sword imposingly. The lines of the fresco are forceful and smooth, showing the character of "the streamer of Wu can prevent wind". The color of the fresco is simple but varied. On the original fresco there are nine people behind, therefore, we can say that this man is the foreman of the guard of honor.

43. Envoys　　On the West Wall of the Passageway　　Height: 128cm, Width 65cm

The figure in the fresco wearing a sharp — topped felt hat, bushy eyebrows, high cheeks, an aquiline nose, full beard, a blue robe with upturned collar, holds a hu (an official tablet) in one hand with the other put at the back. The seams of his clothes are clear and the painting of the moustache is delicate. The painting of the fresco is bold and vigorous. It leaves a strong three — dimentional sense on the audience. The envoy is most probably from an Arabian country. The original fresco of envoy on the west wall of the passageway of the tomb of the crown prince ZhangHuai, Li Xian is damaged. The copy truely depicts one of the envoys in the original fresco. It is precious in history and art.

44. Receiving Foreign Guests　　On the West Wall of the Passageway　　Height: 184.5cm, Width 242.5cm

The three men on the left wear net — like headgears, red court dresses holding hus (official tablets) in their hands. They are the protocol officials of the Hong Lo Si in the Tang Dynasty. The last two on the right, wearing plume crowns, white robes with red collars, wide waistbands, yellow boots, are envoys from Korea. The third one on the right, bald but with heavy eyebrows and sunken eyes, an aquiline nose and a big mouth, wearing a purple robe with upturned collar, is the envoy from the Eastern Rome. The first one on the right may be the envoy from the minority nationality in the northeast of China. The owner of the tomb used to be in charge of the military affairs as a crown princess. The fresco confirms the idea in history, but also provides a true record of the friendly communication of China with her neighbours.

45. The Dancing Maid　　On the North Side of the East Wall of the Front Chamber　　Height: 163cm, Width: 175cm

On the right side of the tree is the maid wearing a red robe a pair of stripped trousers and a pair of sharp — headed shoes. She raises her left sleeve high, places her right hand at her back, tilts her shoulders and twists her back, dancing gracefully. The maid on the left wears a high coil on her head, a white shirt and a green skirt, a yellow shawl, and a pair of square — headed shoes, follows closely. She stretches her right hand forward to beat time. The maid on the right wears a high hair coil on her head, tight and short sleeved shirt, yellow skirt, with her chest uncovered, carries the shawl with her hands, stretches her two arms, bends her back and takes in her abdomen, standing in profile.

46. Two Maidservants　　On the North Wall of the Front Chamber　　Height: 169cm, Width: 106cm

On the right side of the tree stand two maidservants with their backs against each other. The one in the front, with a high hair coil on her head, is very fat. She cups her two hands and places them in front of her chest and turns her head to peep at something. The one at the back, with her hair done in double coils, is slender. She crosses her hands before her chest.

47. Two Maidservants Carrying Musical Instruments　　On the

East Wall of the Front Corridor   Height: 168cm, Width: 117. 5cm

On either side of the vertical stone stands a maid wears a high coil on her head, a tight – sleeved shirt, a long skirt and a pair of tablet – headed shoes. The one on the left holds clappers with her right hand and turns back to call someone. The one on the right carries the bag of piba follows slowly and obediently.

48. A Maidservant Carrying a Jug   On the East Wall of the Front Corridor   Height: 168cm, Width: 119cm

Both of the two maids are dressed in light green tight – sleeved shirt sand yellow skirts. The maid at the back wears a red shawl wrapped round her crossed arms. She stands there gracefully as if she was in deep thought. The front one wears a green shawl which is draped over her left arm. With a jug in her right hand, she is looking over her shoulders at her companion. The fresco exploits the implicit painting method to depict the graceful back of a lady. It gives much food for thought.

49. The Maidservant in Men's Costume Carrying a Potted Landscape   On the East Wall of the Front Tunnel   Height: 119cm

The maidservant has delicate features. She wears a turnban – hat, a round collar long robe, tight trousers, and a pair of sharp – headed shoes. She stands there carrying a potted landscape with her two hands skillfully. It was very popular for women to be dressed in men's costumes in the Tang Dynasty.

50. Three Maidservants Looking up and Holding Objects in Their Hands   On the West Wall of the Front Tunnel   Height: 127cm, Width: 198cm

The three maidservants all have their hair done in a shape of high coil. They wear tight – sleeved shirts. The maidservant on the left with a round and smooth face, is very plump. She wears a low – necked corset with her breasts exposed, a light yellow long skirt. She holds one end of the shawl with her right hand and looks up with all attention with her lefthand over her forehead. The depiction of the posture is vivid and lively. The maidservant in the middle wears a green long skirt, a shawl a pair of red cloud tablet – shaped shoes, carrying a pot with a handle with her two hands facing the cockcombs in blossom. The maid on the right wears a long purple skirt, a red shawl hanging down between her two arms, carrying an object with her two hands, as if she looked back at her companion when walking.

51. The Maidservant Looking Up

52. The Maidservant Carrying a Pot

53. The Maidservant Carrying an Object

54. Three Maidservants Carrying Flower Basins   On the West Wall in the Front Tunnel   Height: 127cm, Width: 198cm

All the three maids with their hair done in a shape of high coil, wear tight – sleeved shirts, yellow skirts, and green shawls. The maid in the middle is plump. She carries a flower basin in the shape of lotus, with a yellow handkerchief under it with her two hands. The red flowers and the green leaves of the flowers in the basin grow luxuriantly. The maidservant on the right, is very pretty with a high nose, a small mouth. She carries the object to the side of her shoulder, twists her waist to look around. The maid on the left is of short and heavy built. She pulls the shawl to her chest with her right hand and holds the lower ends of the shawl with her left hand following closely.

55. The Maid Looking Sideways

56. A Maidservant and a Waiting Man   On the East Wall of the Back Tunnel.   Height: 120cm

On the left is the waiting man. The maidservant standing beside is of tall and fat built. She wears a high coil on her head, with a round face, red lips and turns to look sideways. She looks to be the foreman of the maidservants. The maid in the middle is decking herself out. The maid on the right, with an elliptic face, a straight nose, a small mouth, wears a white tight – sleeved shirt, a long skirt and a yellow shawl. She carries a xiao(a bamboo flute) in box with her hands. The green flourishing bamboos beside add to the quietness, peace and beauty of the environment.

57. The Maidservant Holding a Xiao(A Bamboo Flute)

58. A Foreman and a Maid Decking Herself Out

59. The Waitingmen   On the East Wall of the Back Tunnel Height: 120cm

Both of the two waiting men wear turban – hats, round – collared long robe sand black boots. The one in the front hold an official tablet with his two hands and the one at the back follows closely with his hands cupped.

Prince Yide's Tomb   Tang (706AD)

60. Fortress Towers   On the West Wall of the Passageway Height: 298cm, Width: 302cm

The fresco is the miniature of the cemetery of the master of the tomb. The three main buildings (one big and two small)are build on the trapezoidal base built of bricks. The edges and the corners of the base are covered by stone blocks carved with lines of honeysuckle and there is a certain reduction in the girth. The building is palace like. There are hawk tails on the top of the buildings. The eaves of the buildings all stretch out. There are three rooms in the front and three rooms in the depth. The whole building is surrounded by a corridor. There are five sets of dou gong on the columns. The base is connected with the walls of the cemetery. The background of the tower is the scene of remote mountains and forests.

61. 62. 63. Guards of Honour(Part Ⅰ Part Ⅱ Part Ⅲ))   On the West Wall of the Passageway   Height: 326, 323, 328cm, Width: 224, 239, 227cm

The fresco depicts the scene of the guard of honour when the crownprince goes to court. The guard of honour is composed of chariots, riders and soldiers, three parts. All the people and horses are waiting in lines solemnly and all the chariots are arrayed in order, and all the banners and flags flutter in wind. The sight is majestic and magnificent.

64. Leopard Taming   On the East Wall of the First Corridor Height: 192cm

The fresco is one of the series of frescoes of leopard taming. The tamer wears a turban – hat, a round – collared long robe, a waistband a small bag tied to his waist and a pair of long boots. He carries the taming whip on his left shoulder and leads the spotted leopard with his right hand. The leopard is strong and vigorous with its fur shinning in the sunlight. It is very vigilant. It drags its tail and walks together with its master in the garden. In Tang Dynasty the uniting leopard is the contribution given to the imperial court by the Western Regions. When tamed, it is specially used by the nobles in the imperial court for hunting.

65. Shouldering a Sparrow Hawk and Playing with a Dog   On the West Wall of the Second Corridor   Height: 168cm, Width: 133cm

The picture is only the right half of the original fresco. Beside the tree stands an imperial waiting man, wearing a turban – hat, a round – collaredlong robe and a black belt. With the sparrow hawk standing on his left arm he gesticulates with his right hand and turns back to look around. The yellow hound with a chain around his neck, with his tail turning up tease his master by resting his front paw on his thigh. It is very vigilant and nimbly. The fresco demonstrates the scene in which hound and hawk are tamed at that time.

66. Two Palace Maids　　On the East Side of the South Wall in the Front Chamber　　Height：176cm, Wdith：115cm

The front palace maid with her hair done in a high coil, wears a red tight – sleeved shirt, a purple long skirt, a green shawl and a pair of cloud – shaped shoes with her hands wrapped with the shawl crossed before her chest. The one at the back wears her hair in double ring coils and is dressed in a green tight – sleeved shirt, a red shawl and a long skirt, with a beads – string in her hands. The sketch lines of the fresco can be seen clearly. Although the coloration and the painting of the lines are not completed yet the reserve and the quietness of them are fully depicted in the picture.

67.68. Maid of Honour with Fan　　On the West Wall of the Third Corridor　　Height：166cm, Width：129cm

On either side of the vertical stone stands a palace maid with her hair done in a high coil, in a tight – sleeved shirt, a long skirt, a shawl and a pair of cloud – headed shoes holding a round fan with her two hands. The colors of their skin are different and their facial expressions are also different. They are the both the female officials in charge of banquet in the imperial palace. When copying the original fresco is divided into two parts.

Wei Jiong's Tomb　　Tang（708AD）

69. The Waitingman with a Hun Bottle　　On the North Wall of the Chamber　　Height：70cm, Width：43cm

The waiting man wears a black turban – hat, a red shirt covered with a yellow robe with a color collar. He has broad eyebrows and star like eyes, double – fold eyelids, a high nose and red lips and an upturning chain. He holds a Hun bottle in his arms. The coloration of the picture is appropriate, the lines are accurate and vigorous. It well depicts the formand the image. It is a successful portrait of man .

70. The Waitingmaid with a High Hair Coil　　On the West Wall of the Chamber　　Height：94cm, Width：83cm

The maid with a "lofty cloud – shaped hair coil", rosy cheeks, crescent eyebrows and phoenix eyes, a very elegant figure wears a red tight – sleeved shirt, a shawl around her breasts waving backward. She crosses her hands before her abdomen showing the elegant dignifying character.

71. The Waitingmaid　　On the North Wall of the Chamber Height：100cm, Width：92cm

The waitingmaid with her hair done in a spiral coil, has a round face, crescent eyebrows and pretty eyes, rosy cheeks and rouged lips and a plumb figure. She with her breasts exposed, wears a light red tight – sleeved shirt and a dark red shawl. She pulls her shawl with her hands looking sideways. She expresses the feature of quietness and dignity. It is the typical figure of women in the Tang Dynasty.

Wei Hao's Tomb　　Tang（708AD）

72. The Maidservant with Parrot　　On the East Wall of the North

Mouth of the Back Corridor　　Height：80cm, Width：42cm

The maidservant with double Y – shaped hair coils, is of fine and delicate features. She wears the popular Hun style robes with black belt tied to her waist. A sparrow in front of her turns back her head to look at her master.

73. The Maidservant Feeding a Bird　　On the West Wall of the Back Chamber　　Height：130cm, Width：65cm

The maidservant wears a turban – hat, a long robe with upturned collar, Persian trousers, and soft everyday shoes. The collar of her robe and the edges of the front of her robe are trimmed with beautiful laces. She carries a bird cage with her right hand and feeds the canary standing on her shoulder in a carefree and leisurely manner. The subject matter is lively and interesting.

74. The Maidservant Holding a Cattail Leaf Fan　　On the East Wall of the Back Chamber　　Height：128.5cm, Width：65cm

The maidservant with a spiral coil on her head is very pretty and charming. She wears a yellow tight – sleeved shirt , a red skirt and a green gauze shawl. She holds a cattail leaf fan walking forward slowly. An oriole is flying over on the upper right.

75. High – minded Men　　On the East Wall of the Front Chamber　　Height：170cm, Width：260cm

The three High – minded Men are walking among the pine trees, the stones and the bamboos with bamboo hats on their heads and in red wide – sleeved robes. The one on the right is walking alone with his hands cupped. The two on the left are making gestures with their hands as if they are chatting. The three are separated by pine trees, flowers and stones. They can become independent pictures. The flying red crowned crane, the egret and the canary overhead adds to the quietness and peace of the environment. It looks as if it was a paradise. It shows that the master of the tomb is striving for the leisurely and casual spiritual life.

76. The Maidservant Watching a Bee　　On the West Wall of the North Mouth of the Corridor　　Height：76cm, Width：60cm

The maidservant with her hair done in a shape of spiral coil has crescent eyebrows and pretty eyes, a straight nose, a small mouth and rouged lips. She, with her hands wrapped with the green shawl crossed in front of her abdomen, watches a low – flying bee quietly, with a dragonfly flying over her head.

77. The Flower, the Bird and the Maidservant　　On the South Wall of the Back Chamber　　Height：90.5cm, Width：65cm

The maid wears s spiral hair coil on her head, a yellow tight – sleeved shirt, a green shawl staring at the flowers in full blossom in front of her with a canary flying overhead. What a picture of appreciating the singing bird and the fragrant flowers in the spring season it is.

Madam Xue's Tomb　　Tang（710AD）

78. The Maidservant with Double Ring Hair Coils　　On the West Wall of the Tunnel　　Height：112.5cm, Wdith：47.5cm

The maidservant with double hair coils on her head, has an oval face, worm like eyebrows and phoenix eyes, lightly powdered cheeks, and thinly rouged lips looking sidelong. She wears an orange shirt and a blue gauze skirt. She holds her shawl to the front of her abdomen bending down to look around, expressing a kind of loveliness and childishness.

Zhang Quyi's Tomb　　Tang（748AD）

79. Male Musician　　On the East Wall of the Chamber　Height：44cm, Wdith：63cm

The original fresco has been spoiled. It should be the sight of many musicians sitting on their knees playing musical instruments. Now we can seen the whole sight through one musician. He has the characters of a Mongolian. He has "八" – shaped eyebrows, a high nose, prominent cheek bones and curly beard. He wears a turban – hat, a long robe, a waist belt , sittingon his knees on the ground, holding a long bamboo flute, with his shoulders raised and his eye opened wide blowing with all his efforts. It is vivid and true to life and full of artistic appeal.

Qingshansi Ruin　　Tang(741AD)

80. Buddhist Monks　　On the West Wall of the Room　Height：65cm, width：94cm

Five buddhist monks in the picture in kasayas sitting on the carpet with their legs crossed appreciating music and dance. The one in the front has deep – set eyes, a high nose representing the figure of a Hun watching the performance attentively. Among the other monks, some of them are clapping their hands to the rhythms some are deeply absorbed in the performance. They are all immersed in the wonderful music. There are flowers and grass painted around.

81. Musicians　　On the West Wall of the Room　　Height：69cm, Width：107.5cm

There are ten female musicians in the picture. All of them wear tassels around their hair coils chains and arm bracelets , with their breasts and abdomens exposed. Nine of them sit on the carpet with their legs crossed holding a horizontal flute, a piba, a sheng, a pair of clappers a pai xiao and other musical instruments in their hands playing ensembles attentively. The dancer in the front waves the silk ribbon whirling softly and gracefully.

Su Sixu's Tomb　　Tang(745AD)

82.83 Huteng Music and Dance　　On the East Wall of the Chamber　　Height：142, 148cm, Width：147, 137cm

The original fresco is divided into three pieces when taken off. The copy is about the orchestra on the left and the dancer in the middle. There are six musicians in the band three of whom in the front row hold a piba, a sheng (a reed pipe wind instrument) and the cymbals respectively. Of the three in the back row one is the conductor, another is blowing a horizontal flute and the third one is beating time with the clappers. The dancer has bushy eyebrows, a high nose and curly beard. He wears a white towel around his head a round collar robe, a waist leather belt and a pair of black boots. According to the archaeological research, this style of dancing is derived from HUTENG dance of the Western Regions. It is the precious material for the study of music and dance in the Tang Dynasty.

84. Palace Maid　　On the North Wall of the Chamber　Height：149cm, Width：66cm

The hair on the lady's two temples comes down to cover her cheeks, and the bun – shaped hair on top of her head inclines forward. She has a round and smooth face, fine and delicate features, with cosmetics on her cheeks , with her nose and lips well proportioned expressing quietness and grace. She wears a wide collar front – intersected garment, with a shawlwrapping her shoulders and hanging down with both her hands cupped before her chest. She has a full figure and decorous appearance. This is the typical image of a lady of the Tang Dynasty.

Nanliwang – cun　　Tomb (8th Century)

85. Scarlet Bird　　On the South Wall of the Chamber　　Height：130cm, Width99cm

The Scarlet Bird symbolizes the Southern Supernatural Being in ancient China. It is often found in the paintings of Tang tombs to indicate directions. In the picture the bird with a long beak, eagle like eyes, raises its head and spreads its wings to tent to fly high into the sky with floating clouds around. The colors are fresh and the lines are bold and vigorous and true to life.

86. The Xuan Wu　　On the North Wall of the Chamber　　Height：170cm, Width：100cm

It is a joint body of a tortoise and a snake representing the Northern Supernatural Being in ancient China. It is often found to be painted in tombs to indicate directions. As is shown in the picture the tortoise with a long neck a round body and strong feet lies below and the snake twines round the body of the tortoise with its head and tail intersecting to form a ring. The tortoise and the snake are glaring at each other and with their mouths widely open face to face. The floating clouds are flying around.

87. A Picnic Outside　　On the East Wall of the Chamber　Height：180cm, Width：235cm

In the middle of the picture is placed a rectangular table on which there are cups and dishes. On the wooden block in front of the table lies a lotus – shaped soup pot and a ladle with a crooked handle. On each of the three couches around the table are seated three diners who wear turban – hats and long robes, chatting happily and drinking cheerfully. Among all the diners some are whispering to each other, some are clapping their hands to add to the fun, some are appreciating the food and the wine, some are clinking each other's cups. It is full of enjoyment and liveliness. On either side of the table stands a young girl with her hair worn in two coils carrying a tray with five on – lookers surrounding. Their different expressions are lively and lifelike. The background of the picture is the flowing clouds. The bold and natural painting style is similar to the freehand brushwork in Chinese painting. With the protruding personalities of the characters painted in the picture it is really a vivid valuable historical custom picture.

Princess Tangan's Tomb　　Tang(784AD)

88. Flowers and Birds　　On the West Wall of the Chamber　Height：180cm, Width：380cm

There is a wood basin with a round opening and a round stem in the middle. The outside of the basin is painted black and decorated round – shaped flowers. There are four birds, namely a turtledove, an oriole, a parriot and a white pigeon standing on the edge of the basin. On the upper left of the basin there are two magpies and on the upper right there is a turtledove flying together. There is a wintersweet on either side of the basin with their tops intersecting each other on the top of the picture. There are tawny diary roses and cockcombs etc. in between. It is fresh and lively and full of temperament and interest. The pictures of flowers and birds are used only as ornaments. They are rarely painted as the main theme of a picture. This picture , so far, is the only known picture of flowers and birds in the Tang Dynasty with exact time record. It provides important research materials for the Chinese art history.

Ningxia Guyuan Area

89. Walking a Horse   In the Sui Danasty (581 - 618)
Height: 88cm, Width: 114cm

The man who is leading the horse wears a round collar robe and a pair of black boots. Holding the reins and a whip with his crossed hands before his chest turns to look sideways. The light brown horse with plump and sturdy body and round buttocks, with short - cut mane and a tied tail , a saddle and saddle cloth on back walks slowly together with his master.

90. Warrior (Part)   In the Sixth Year of Daye in the Sui Dynasty (608) On the East Wall of the Light Well in the Tome of Shi Wu Zhao   The Height of the Figure: 166cm

The warrior has a high nose and deep - set eyes, up - turned mustache and curly beard. He wears a high hat, a wide - sleeved long robe, leaning on the broad knife with a handle with double rings. The figure is vivid and true to life, demonstrating the strong personal characters. Frescoes are rarely found in the tombs of the Sui Dynasty, so it is a very valuable material.

The Mural Painting From the Grottoes In Dunhuang and Xinjiang
Dunhuang Mogao Grottoes

91. An Apsaras   In the Sui Dynasty (581 - 618)   Height: 44cm, Width: 65cm

Two apsaras are flying over the clouds in the sky. The front one is spreading flowers while the one at the back is waving a streamer and flying with fortunate clouds floating around. The sight is very pleasant.

92. Bodhisattva   In the Sui Dyansty (518 - 618)   On the South Side of the Outside of the Shrine In the 404Th Cave Height: 60cm, Width: 46cm

The Bodhisattva , with crescent eyebrows and drooping eyes, wears a flower crown on her head. Her left index finger is picking up a honeysuckle. The posture of her hand is soft and ingenious. It demonstrates delicate beauty and loveliness.

93. Avalokitesvara and Bodhisattva   In the Early Period of the Tang Dynasty (618 - 704) On the East Side of the Skt.. Dharmacakra - Pravartana Fresco In the Middle of the South Wall in the 57th Cave   Height: 100cm, Wodtj: 64cm

The painting of the figure in the picture is very delicate and the figure is very beautiful and graceful. The Skt. Avalokitesvara in the middle wears a flower crown. With a circle of light behind, she is plump and elegant, with thin eyebrows and long eyes, a straight nose and red lips. The ornaments of the crown, the jewelled necklace and strings of ornaments and the arm bracelets are painted with gilt. The decorative patterns of her clothes and ornaments are complicated and beautiful and colorful.

94. To Come Into Being on the Back of an Elephant   In the Early Period of the Tang Dynasty (618 - 704) On the Top of the West Shrine In the 329th Cave   Height: 65cm, Width: 102cm

To come into being on the back of an elephant is one scene when the crown prince Sakaya(Sakayamuni) was born. The white elephant flying through the clouds with his feet stepping on the lotus thrones carried by the naked apsaras in Buddhism. The Bodhisttva, wearing a crown inlaid with jewels , a heaven robe, a long shirt sits on the back of an elephant peacefully with two servants waiting on either side, the front of whom is carrying a

spittoon. The apsaras on dragons are pioneers, and the other apsaras following around. With the rosy clouds floating over, the heaven flowers flying everywhere, the sight is majestic.

95. A Female Maidservant   In the Early Period of Tang Dynasty (618 - 704) On the South Side of the East Wall of the Painting of Skt. Dharmacakra - Pravartana In the 329TH Cave   Height: 98cm, Width: 70cm

The maid, with her hair done in a shape of half moon bun jabbed with a spear - like hairpin ·, a round chubby face, crescent eyebrows and exquisite eyes, a straight nose and a cherry - shaped mouth is dressed in a decollete round collar tight - sleeved shirt, a transparent gauze shawl and a black skirt. She is kneeling on the carpet quietly with her hands holding a lotus. The lines of the picture are concise and the connotation is rich. Though the figure is only 22cm in height, it is considered to be the masterpiece of the servant maids in DUN HUANG frescoes.

96. Bodhisattva   In the Early Deriod of Tang Dynasty   On the North Side of the Painting of The Stopy of Vimalakirti In the West Thrine In the 334th Cave   Height: 69cm, Width: 46cm

The original fresco was painted in the tent of Vimalakirti. The Bodhisttva, with a crown inlaid with jewels on head, a nimbus behind her chest and shoulders uncovered, bare feet, wears a long skirt, the ornaments of streamers, a necklace, arm bracelets, holding an alms bowl in her hands, kneeling on the lotus throne, looking up at something piously. The picture is well arranged and colorful.

97. Dancing in Pair   In the Early Period of the Tang Dynasty(618 - 704)   On the Top of the South Side of the Niche on the West Wall   Height: 64cm, Width: 91cm

The picture takes the blue sky as the background. On the above is painted a Buddha, sitting on the lotus throne with his two disciples floating with the fortune clouds. The double apsaras are flying high in the sky, with the long skirts and colorful ribbons fluttering in the wind. The color is rich and gaudy, and the composition of the picture is wonderful. The six spreading flower heaven people who are graceful overlooks the down world (the earth) along the banisters. It is the wonderful sight of the heaven state.

98. A Pair of Dancers   In the Early Period of the Tang Dynasty (618 - 704) In the Lower Part of the Painting of the Story of Skt. Amitabha on the South Wall In the 220th Cave   Height: 64cm, Width: 91cm

The dancer with naked upper limbs, bare feet, wears a flower crown and a necklace, a thin shawl, a pair of black trousers, a pomegranate - shaped skirt, arm bracelets with bronze bells, wave color ribbons with her two hands revolving on the small round carpet in the shape of a standing golden pheasant. The dance is lively and bold.

99. Female Donor   In the Prosperous Period of the Tang Dynasty (705 - 780) On the South Side of the East Wall in the 225th Cave In Dun Huang Grottoes   Height: 76cm, Width: 50cm

The maidservant wears a red chief on her head, a red shirt covered with a white robe with green lace holding a silver ware with a folding handle with her two hands, kneeling on the ground piously. The lines of the picture are concise and the colors of the picture are plain and graceful.

100. Vimalakirti In the Prosperous Period of the Tang Dynasty

(705 – 780) Part of the Painting of the Story of Skt. Vimalakirti on the South Side of the East Wall in the 103rd Cave   Height: 94cm, Width:64cm

He, with a soft a scarf around his head, in white robe covered by red cloak with black edges, with bare feet, sitting on the Hun bed, with his body inclined forward a little bit, waves a horsetail duster with one of his hands. He, raising his eyebrows high and opening his mouth wide, raises overbearing questions to the contestant. The lines are vigorous, and the density of the colors is well organized. It depictsthe wisdom and far sightedness and the glibness of a lay Buddhist. It is one of the masterpieces of the portraits of people in Mo Gao grottoes.

101. Deva – musician and Donor   In the Middle Period of the Tang Dynasty (781 – 847) in the Lower Part of the Painting of the Story of Manjusri on the North Side of the West Wall In the 159th Cave   Height:88cm, Width:66cm

Three musicians of the heaven are playing musical instruments attentively. The one in the middle is beating a pair of clappers. The one on the left is blowing a flute. And the one on the right is blowing a shen(a multi – piped flute).

102. Servant Bodhisattvas   In the Middle Period of the Tang Dynasty (781 – 847) Part of the Painting of the Story of Manjusri In the 159th Cave   Height:43cm, Width36cm

The three servant Bohisttvas wear flower crowns, earrings, necklaces, arm bracelets, trousers – like skirts, silk shawls. They, with naked upper limbs, bare feet, hold alms bowls, Skt. amarta – kalasas, flowers, sitting on their knees on the lotus throne. They are all of fine and delicate features, sedate and elegant. Their bodies are just like jade, full of youthful vigour.

103. Samantabhadra   In the Middle Period of the Tang Dynasty (781 – 847) In the Painting of the Story of Skt. Samantabhadra In the 159th Cave   Height:100cm, Width:63cm

She has a round face, long ears, crescent eyebrows and drooping eyes, red lips and mustache. She, dressed in colorful clothes and ornaments, is very elegant. She carries a flower in her left hand sitting on the elephant – shaped throne with her legs crossed. The colors of the picture are quietly elegant, and the lines are subtle representing a very high artistic level.

104. Bodhisattva   In the Middle Period of the Tang Dynasty   (781 – 847) On the North Side of the West Thrine In the 199th Cave   Height:124.5cm, Width:50cm

She, being of tall and heavy built, has a round and chubby face, sparce eyebrows and bright eyes, and a circle of light behind. She, with her chest uncovered, wears a crown inlayed with jewels, eardrops, a necklace, arm bracelets, a shawl and a skirt. She carries a vase with flowers with her right hand, standing on the lotus throne with bare feet. The folds of her clothes are subtle; the expression of the figure is full of radiating vigour; the lines are forceful and the color is soft reflecting a kind of new painting style in Mo Go caves in the middle period of the Tang Dynasty.

105. An Apsaras   In the Late Period of the Tang Dynasty (7TH – 9TH Century) Part of the Painting of the Story of Nirvana on the West Wall In the 158th Cave   Height:84cm, Width61.5cm

The apsara, holding a jeweled necklace in her hand, has a high coil on her head, a forehead bracelet, a roud face, big ears, thin eyebrows and drooping eyes. She wears a green skirt, a pair of brown trousers colorful shawl, with her upper limbs exposed . She has the ornaments of eardrops, a necklace, arm bracelets, and

waist bracelets. She holds up her head and throws out her chest, twists her waist floating over the clouds in the sky, showing a soft and graceful posture. On the upper part a goose is flying with a lotus flower in its mouth.

106. Servant Bodhisattva   In the Late Period of the Tang Dynasty (848 – 906) Part of the Painging of the Story of Bhaisajyaguruon the North Wall In the 220th Cave   Height: 58cm, Width:37.5cm

She wears a forehead bracelet inlaid with pearls, arm bracelets, waist bracelets, breast ornaments, a pair of trousers with ridge squares and a silk shawl. She, with her upper limbs exposed, kneels on the lotus throne by the pond with her left hand holding a flower bud, raising her head high to stare at the statue of Bhaisajyaguru. In the pond a pair of mandarin ducks are playing gaily in the water, presenting a true and fresh and lively atmosphere.

107. Hunting   In the Late Period of the Tang Dyansty (848 – 906) Part of the Painting of Zhang Yi Chao In a Procession on the Lower Layer of the Souty Side of the East Wall In the 156th Cave   Height:44.4cm, Width:59.5cm

The remote mountains set off the extensiveness of the champaign in the picture. The small deer and fox are so frightened that they are running away by all means in all directions. Two hunters are chasing them on horse backs violently, with arrow on the stretched bows. The tenseness of hunting scene is vividly shown on the wall.

108. Nandikesvara   In the Yuan Dynasty(13 – 14th Centuary) In the 465th Cave   Height:64cm, Width:48.5cm

The picture takes the Esoteric Sect as its subject matter. It is one of the double – body statues manifested by Sakyamni to control the world of desires. The main statue is blue grey, wearing a silver helmet, an apron, a string of skull ornaments around his neck. He has three eyes and six arms. Among the six arms two of them are holding the mother of Buddha. The mother of Buddha, being yellowish pink color, with a high coil, a forehead bracelet, naked completely, holds the neck of the main statue with her two arms, with her left leg resting on the right leg of the main statue. The color of the picture is soft and the effect of the picture is reverse.

Dunhuang Yulin Grottoes

109. The Southern Lokapala   In the Tang Dynasty (7 – 9th Century) On the South Side of the East Wall In the 15th Cave Height:91cm, Width:68cm

The Southern Lokapala wears colorfully painted helmets and armour, a pair of battle boots, a cloak, colorful ribbons, a waistband with animal faces. Behind his head is a ring of flame and shining light. He holds an arrow in his hand, with a bow tied to his waist, sitting on the shoulders of two devils with hard and firm fleshes, full of power, grandeur and refinement, with a small devil holding a fan in his hands, an apsara flying overhead.

110. Donors   (10th Century)   Height:117cm, Width:79cm

In the front row are four noble women, wearing flower ornaments and gold hairpins on their heads, with their hair on their temples going down to cover their cheeks, with thick cosmetics on their faces, put on coin – like ornaments and draw flowers. Dressed in silks and satins ornamented with pearls and jewels, they stand their piously with their hands cupped. According to the label with the title of the picture in the long rectangular frame, they are the late new ladies of a certain noble family. The are the figures of the two new ladies and their nephews. The four maidservants are standing in two rows. Two of them are holding round fans in their hands.

Kezier Grottoes

111. The Rhombus Check and the Picture of Jataka   In the Jin Dynasty the South and the North Imperial Period 3rd - 6th Century) Part of the East Side of the Vaulted Ceiling of the Main Cave In the 38th Cave   Height: 44.5cm, Width:61cm

The rhombus check paintings are one of the extraordinary artistic characteristics of the frescoes in Gui Zi. In almost all the Ke Zier caves are painted rhombus check frescoes. On the left and the right of the painting are the stories of Jatakas.

112. Jataka Story (Tales of the Buddha's Previous Lives)   In the Jin Dynasty - The South and the North Imperial Period (3rd - 6th Century) In the 17th Cave   Height:63cm, Width:43cm

In the rhombus check painting, the theme of the macque using his body to set up a bridge is depicted. The lawn is dotted with some round flowers. At the bottom is painted a small river, on either side of which stands a tree. One white macaque holds the trunks of the trees with his front and rear paws, to stretch his body to set up the bridge. Two macaques, one of which blue and the other one is black, walk on his body to cross the river. Another white macque stands on the northside of the bank of the river to receive them. On the above of the rhombus check there is a tree.

113. Rhoumbus Jataka Paintings and the Jataka Painting   In the Jin Dyansty (- The South and the North Imperial Period (3rd - 6th Century) Part of the South Side on the Vaulted Ceiling In 38th Cave   Height: 44.5cm, Width:61cm

On the left of the fresco is Si Wang Jataka. He has contributed his body to Brahamana and follows with his hands tied by himself. On the right is the Wen Jie Jataka. with half of the naked jumping down from the trees and a yaksa standing beside.

114. Dancing Maid   In the South and North Imperial Period (5th - 6th Century) In the 8th Cave   Hegiht:98cm, Width:65cm

In the rhombus check is painted a completely naked dancer tan talizing the Buddhist. The dancer is clump, taking in her chest and twisting her thigh in a artificial manner, presenting the feeling of human being. It is one of the masterpieces of the portraits of human body.

115.Jataka Story (Tales of the Buddha's Previous Lives)   In the Tang Dynasty In the 118th Cave   Hegith:45cm, Width:78cm

In the rhombus a female musician is playing the ruan (atraditional Chinese string musical instrument). All the birds around are flying and singing to the soft and sweet tune. The sight is peaceful and auspicious.

116. Deva - Musicians   In the South and North Imperial Period (5th - 6th Century) On the Top of the Main Cave In the 8th Cave

Height:109cm, Width:82cm

The background of the painting is purple inlaid with white pebblestones, on which are painted two female musicians. The front one is white and the black one is white. But both of them have a circle of light behind them and wear waist bracelets, and streamers. The one in the front wears a crown with pearls, a pair of green trousers, holdinga piba with her two hands, twisting her waist and turning her thigh to make her body in a form of an arch, with the two feet to cross. The one at the back holds a flower tray in either hand. The harmony and the integral of the density of the colors and the lines of the strong sense of "coming out of the wall" on the audience.

117. Buddha and Gandharva   In the Jin Dyansty - the South — the North Imperial Period (The 3rd - 6th Century) In the 13th Cave   Height:153cm, Width:93cm

It depicts the story of Buddha and Grandharva. He is the god of entertainment of the eight gods, who is unrestrained and disrespectful to Buddhism. The Buddhist is the incarnation to compete with him to play kong hou (an ancient plucked stringed instrument). He feels that he is not competent, so he revolt against Buddhism. The one standing on the right in the picture is Buddha holding a kong hou. The one on the left with white skin, and naked completely is the incarnation of the god of music standing there with his feet crossed. He rests one of his shoulders on the shoulders of Grandharva. The expression is soft and quiet, presenting the life of the human world.

118. Buddha and Gandharva (Part)

Kumutula Grottoes

119. Bodhisattva   In the North Imperial (4 - 6th Century) In the 21st Cave   Height:88.5, Width:62cm

On the dome of the cave there are 13 pictures of Bodihisttvas arranged in a radiating manner. This is one of them. The Bodhisattva has a round face, big ears, crescent eyebrows and linear eyes, a straight nose and thick lips, tadpole mustache on her upper lip, curly hair hanging down to her shoulders. She wears a crown with jewels, a necklace, tassels, arm bracelets, and an redish color skirt. She holds a waistband inlaid with pearls and jade, presenting a graceful and beautiful posture. The figure is clump; the lines are forceful and the colors are fresh, fully representing the artistic style of the Gui Zi nationality in the ancient time.

Turpan Bozikelik Grottoes

120. Deva - Musician   In the Yuan Dynasty (13 - 14th Century) In the 54th Cave   Height:76cm, Width:52cm

The musician wears a crown with flowers, a shawl and skirt, with her upper limbs uncovered, and bare feet. On her neck, arms, wrists and ankles are bracelet ornaments. She has a round and chubby face, a straight nose and red lips, crescent eyebrows and drooping eyes, sitting on a round carpet with her legs crossed holding a kong hou in her hands.

編　　撰:李國珍
責任編輯:魏明道
美術策劃:魏明道　石頭娃　沈健康
英文翻譯:周五龍　秦改進　李貴倉
攝　　影:羅忠民
Compiled by Li Guozhen
Edited by Wei Mingdao
Art Designed by Wei Mingdao Shi Touwa Shen Jiankang
Translated by Zhou Wulong, Qin Gaijin, Li Guicang
Photographed by Luo Zhongmin

大唐壁畫

MAGNIFICENT FRESCOS FROM THE GREAT TANG DYNASTY

陝新登字012號
出版:中國·陝西旅游出版社(西安市長安路32號)
承印:天時印刷(深圳)有限公司
發行:中國·陝西新華書店經銷
開本:889×1194(毫米)1/16印張:10.5
書號:ISBN7-5418-1332-X/J·242
1996年8月第1版第1次印刷0188
版權所有　不得翻印

Shaanxi Publishing Bureau of information register number:012
Publish:China Shaanxi Tourism Publishing House
Printed By:Tims Printing (shen zhen) Co.,Ltd
Issue:China Shaanxi Tourism Publishing House Sold by China
　　　Shaanxi Book Stop
Format:889×1194(㎜)1/16 page:10.5
Number:ISBN 7-5418-1332-X/J·242
August:1996 First Edition 0188